CORRESPONDENCE

PIERRE TEILHARD DE CHARDIN

MAURICE BLONDEL

CORRESPONDENCE

With Notes and Commentary
By Henri de Lubac, S.J.

Translated by William Whitman

HERDER AND HERDER

1967
HERDER AND HERDER NEW YORK
232 Madison Avenue, New York 10016

Original Edition: *Blondel et Teilhard de Chardin*
Paris, Beauchesne, 1965

Nihil obstat: Brendan W. Lawlor, Censor Deputatus
Imprimatur: Patrick C. Brennan, Vicar General
March 8, 1967

Library of Congress Catalog Card Number 67–17627
© 1967 by Herder and Herder, Inc.
Manufactured in the United States

Contents

CORRESPONDENCE

CORRESPONDENCE

Preface

Dating from the year 1899, Fr. Auguste Valensin (September 12, 1879—December 18, 1953) corresponded on a regular basis[1] with Maurice Blondel, formerly his professor and now his friend. He liked to call upon the older man's judgment and enjoyed showing him the work of his colleagues. He also maintained a long exchange of letters with Fr. Pierre Teilhard de Chardin (May 1, 1881—April 10, 1955), a fellow Jesuit and native of the province of Lyons.

Pierre Teilhard and Auguste Valensin were novices together in Aix-en-Provence. The former entered his novitiate on March 20, 1899, the latter joining him there in October of the same year, after receiving his degree in philosophy in Aix under Blondel. Later they studied literature and philosophy together at Jersey, then spent two years at Ore Place, in Sussex near the town of Hastings, where they studied theology. In the years to come Pierre Teilhard often appealed to Auguste Valensin for advice in matters of a personal nature. He considered him a true "spiritual father," as a number of his letters testify. On learning of his death, Fr. Teilhard wrote from New York to his cousin Marguerite Teillard, "It was Valensin who taught me how to think. I could tell him everything, and though we rarely said so, we loved each other deeply. Now he is 'seeing.' When will my turn come?"[2]

After his discharge from the service, Fr. Teilhard de Chardin spent part of the summer of 1919 at Jersey, where his friend had just begun—and was soon to discontinue—lecturing on the history of philosophy. He also found Fr. Pierre Charles there, a mutual friend from their Hastings days, and had a number of

9

visits with him. Fr. Charles had been appointed professor of theology at the Jesuit College in Louvain in 1914.[3] It was he who was to work with such persistence towards the publication of *The Divine Milieu*. As we know, this project did not materialize.[4] Through his short, widely read book *Prière de toutes les heures* he did manage to introduce readers to several of the ideas central to Teilhard's spiritual position. And later, in the years following World War II, he was to go to great lengths to defend his friend and to impress others with the vital urgency of his work. That summer of 1919 found him completing a short essay on deductive ontology. Auguste Valensin had no great liking for it, and it increased Pierre Teilhard's instinctive wariness of "metaphysics." But when Teilhard began "Mon univers" in 1924 (the second essay with that title) and wrote on the first page, "I have found exceptional friends to help me begin my thought,"[5] he was certainly thinking of Fr. Charles, along with Auguste Valensin, Victor Fontoynont, and several others.

That summer Fr. Valensin was working on a long article on pantheism which Fr. Adhémar d'Alès had asked him to do for his *Dictionnaire apologétique*.[6] In July and August, Fr. Teilhard tried to persuade him to go beyond the refutation of pantheistic thought-systems by incorporating a second, constructive study into his paper, "an essay synthesizing the Christian faith." Valensin was quite open to the suggestion, in theory at least. He agreed that "the universe forms a natural whole, whose only real existence is suspended to our Lord." This was the "main thing" for Teilhard, who was already hoping that the only areas of disagreement left between them lay in "questions of emphasis or shading." This Pauline conviction was very important to Teilhard. But he knew that if his friend joined him in it, he was doing so "more for the sake of drawing a philosophy together than from a need to revere an omnipresence." This marks the essential difference between the two men, a difference which will show up in their exchanges in the years to follow. However, it did not prevent them from understanding each other. In fact Teilhard found it valuable; "I seem to have found a true friend in Valensin," he confided to his cousin Marguerite, "all the truer in that he isn't absolutely with me in my train of thought, despite all his openness and intellectual sympathy for me."[7]

He asked Valensin to read "Mon univers," an essay written in 1918, and an important text in that it was his first attempt at a spiritual autobiography. "[In these pages]," he writes, "I have tried to define the original, fundamental elements of my vision of the world, so that I might clarify my own doctrine to myself, and so that I might lighten the task of criticism and reorientation for those whose right it is to guide me."[8] He also showed him the "three stories in the style of Benson" which he wrote in October of 1916, just before going up to Douaumont, and possibly a number of the other essays he wrote during the war, and of course the two texts he had just finished at Jersey,[9] "The Spiritual Power of Matter" with its final "Hymn," and "eight pages on the way we might properly think of the limits of the human body."[10]

That summer they often spoke of two men, Maurice Blondel and Fr. Pierre Rousselot, who had been killed in Les Eparges in the spring of 1915 at the age of thirty-seven. Both Valensin and Teilhard had known Rousselot well and had been strongly influenced by him. They were still shaken by his death—and would be disturbed on his account again soon when they were to learn of the decree issued in Rome in August of 1920 proscribing the teaching of his doctrine "The Eyes of Faith" in the theological colleges of the Society.[11] His writings were keen and extremely rich in thought, and were in Valensin's possession for safekeeping. Blondel had had "mixed feelings" of pleasure and irritation with Rousselot's famous thesis on *L'Intellectualisme de saint Thomas d'Acquin;* it had been presented at the Sorbonne in 1908. The two had since reached an understanding, however, for they had struck up an exchange, Valensin acting as their intermediary, and Rousselot fell under the professor's influence to some extent.[12]

In that very month, August 1919, Valensin received a letter from Aix dealing with "The Eyes of Faith" and with the article

11

on pantheism, which was then in the gestation stage. The thought occurred to both friends that they might submit Teilhard's work to Blondel for criticism. Probably Valensin voiced the idea first, with an enthusiasm that may have been tinged with some anxiety. Teilhard, for his part, was quite taken by the proposal. Valensin was in the habit of spending several months of the year in Aix, and when he left Jersey in mid-September, he took several of Teilhard's manuscripts with him. On September 18 he wrote to Blondel from Paris,

"I'm making my way to Aix in short hops. I say 'to Aix' but what I mean is, to you. How much I have to tell you! I'd like to show you two or three short pieces which one of my closest friends, Father Teilhard de Chardin, has written on the relationship between Christ and the cosmos. He is a geologist by training, and is preparing a doctor's degree in Paris where he will occupy a professorial chair already reserved for him. But he also has philosophical views and we would both be gratified if you would look at them and give them your appraisal."

On September 22 Blondel replied, "I'll be pleased to look into the various works you mentioned."

We do not have an actual list of the essays submitted to Maurice Blondel. Fr. Teilhard had written twenty or so in the space of four years (1916–1919). Twenty are in print today, collected in the volume *Ecrits du temps de la guerre* (1965). They are in varying measure philosophical, apologetic, and spiritual. In the letter we cited a moment ago, Father Valensin spoke of "two or three short pieces." "Mon univers" and "The Spiritual Power of Matter" would certainly be among them, as well as several others, no doubt, for Blondel is to speak of "various essays." But it is unlikely that Teilhard had all his writings with him at Jersey, and one would assume that neither he nor Valensin would have wanted to burden Blondel with an unmanageable amount of material.

The correspondence which Valensin initiated between the two men was to be followed up in a more direct fashion. In a letter Teilhard wrote to his friend, dated Paris, February 28,

1920, we read, "If you see Maurice Blondel, tell him I appreciated his last card very much—and please not to feel pressed about replying." Teilhard took his final examination for his doctorate in natural science (zoology), and then, in late March, went to Aix-en-Provence where Valensin introduced him to the philosopher. "I had a long visit with Blondel," he wrote to Marguerite on March 28. To our knowledge, nothing remains of that interview.

Whatever the exact list may have been, the "various essays" submitted to Blondel were echoes of the days which Teilhard had spent in reflection and intense prayer in the course of the war which had just ended. Later, in 1925, and again through Valensin, Blondel was to have the opportunity to see others— the second version of "Mon univers" (1924) and "Pantheisme et Christianisme" (1923); and he would respond to them with the same sympathy and with similar reservations.[13] Towards the end of his long life he praised Teilhard for his "concrete method." Thinking back to his youth, he recalled a talk he had had with Jules Lachelier. In a tone bordering on agony, the famous old man had told him, "How I would love to be able to reconcile Darwin and the Bible!" Now an old man of eighty-six himself, Blondel remarked, "What consolation he would have found in Fr. Teilhard de Chardin's paleontology and serene faith!" (December 26, 1947).[14]

Clearly, Blondel's response to these essays does not represent a final judgment on a work which was just getting under way in 1919, a system of thought which was obviously seeking its own voice—and which was always to be seeking it, more or less.[15] His remarks were made to good effect, even though their main contribution lies in what they have done to make the Teilhardian thought-system clear, rather than in any sort of change they might have produced in the younger man's initial orientation.

The letters we are going to read will teach us as much about one correspondent as about the other, and will show us that despite a rather marked difference in accent and perspective, the two men shared some ideas and were not far apart in others.

13

Blondel may seem to be more Augustinian in his leanings, Teilhard more Thomistic. One feels they had a similar depth of faith, as well as a background of spiritual life which, while not strictly similar, responded sympathetically to the other's, much as an overtone will sound when a note is struck on a lower register. On several delicate but limited points they found there was more a "gap" between them than a real "difference of opinion." Both felt they were in agreement on essentials. In his second paper Maurice Blondel will admit that his initial remarks were "unjustified" at times, and Fr. Teilhard de Chardin, for his part, will be pleased to find that the philosopher's explanations strike a note of "perfect resonance with my own most vital thoughts."

Still, "resonance" is not quite consonance. The reader notices this right away. Here and there we feel that neither of them wants to take a sharp stand against the other, and of course the mediation of Fr. Valensin, their mutual friend and the initiator of the correspondence, tends to promote the irenical element in their exchange. This is not to say, however, that they were not completely open with each other as they discussed this subject which meant so much to them, or that they concealed their innermost selves. Pierre Teilhard, who is always modest, never really speaks "without great hesitation," be it with a striving for clarity of thought—a clarity which is almost cutting, such is his desire for precision. Sometimes Maurice Blondel is less concerned with grasping the detail of his interlocutor's thought than he is with expressing his own—he did have this tendency —here and there using the other's position to throw his own into sharp relief. In any case they both agree, and this time perfectly, that the final answer lies beyond these essays of personal faith, beyond the inevitable partiality of their respective aims; it is found in what Fr. Teilhard calls, by way of conclusion, "the practices of the saints" and the "empirical and complex attitude of the Church." Both of them are seeking Christianity in its fullness and depth.

This exchange will be disappointing to a reader who expects, as is sometimes the case in the official recounting of certain debates, the victory of one party, and the winning over of his opponent. Clearly, neither of the men was able to arrive at a complete picture of where the other stood. Though their problems were similar, they were not identical, nor could they be. Forty years of systematic thought had equipped Blondel with a firm doctrine and had committed him to paths which precluded his fully sharing in the new experience of his junior; —and this experience, being both scientific and spiritual in nature, did not give Fr. Teilhard the thorough grasp of philosophy which was Blondel's. Nevertheless, one could hardly say that a real exchange did not take place. And when one considers the lengths they went to to cultivate a receptive mind to the best in the other, and to extend as much deference as possible to the internal necessities of the other's thought—and this, without the slightest concession or weakening which might have compromised their individual views of the truth—it is an exemplary dialogue.[16]

Notes to Preface

1. Maurice Blondel and Auguste Valensin, *Correspondance* (Paris, 1957–1965, 3 vols.). Auguste Valensin, *Textes et documents inédits* (Paris, 1961).

2. *Letters from a Traveler* (New York and London, 1962), p. 348.* [An asterisk will indicate that the present translator has supplied his own translation for the passage in question.]

3. See *Correspondance,* t. 3, pp. 67–69. Fr. Charles had finished his theological studies at Hastings in 1910. See Pierre Teilhard de Chardin, *Letters from Hastings* (New York and London, 1967), letter 54. After meeting Charles in Brussels in 1926 and discussing a matter of conscience with him, Teilhard wrote: "He gave me the only advice I'm able to understand, but which I must prove worthy of through greater fidelity: you have to bathe that in more light."

4. See Henri de Lubac, *La pensée religieuse du Père Pierre Teilhard de Chardin* (Paris, 1962), pp. 24–25.

5. *Œuvres,* t. 9, p. 66. In the sentence where he speaks of himself "standing at the frontier of two worlds, faced with a choice," he is also referring to his laic friends at the Museum of Natural History.

6. This piece was "circumcised and toned down" before its publication in 1921: "I am humiliated by my article on pantheism. It was already in proof form when I had to cut out three quarters of its substance, reducing it to something of no significance whatever." See Valensin, *Textes et documents inédits,* pp. 133, 146, 153.

7. Letters to Marguerite Teillard-Chambon, the 2nd, 8th, and 28th of August, 1919* (*The Making of a Mind,* New York and London, 1965), pp. 298, 300, 303.

8. Pierre Teilhard de Chardin, *Ecrits du temps de la guerre* (Paris, 1965), p. 267. See letter of August 2, 1919 (*The Making of a Mind,* p. 297).

9. Letters of the 5th and 17th of September, 1919 (*The Making of a Mind,* pp. 306 and 308).

10. Pages which seem to have been lost, though we may have part of them, or a résumé in a text published in *Science et Christ,* pp. 33–35, in the section entitled "En quoi consiste le corps humain."

11. Auguste Valensin, *Textes et documents inédits,* p. 146. Blondel-Valensin, *Correspondance,* t. 3, pp. 72–74, with bibliography. On August 11, 1920, Teilhard wrote to Valensin: "I am exasperated with myself for not having written you sooner. I am sharing in the inner, spiritual suffering you have been going through these last two weeks. Know that my sympathies are with you, and that now, yes, now more than ever, I bless the Providence which put you and Charles in my path, and that I do so without rancor or reproach. — Time and obedience will yield a clearer picture of the immortal and essentially Christian elements in the ideas which have been censured. I know that they are my support, that I couldn't nourish my mind or sustain my faith without them. —There are many others who feel as I do. —Therefore—should you (by any remote chance) have been led to wonder whether your influence on me has been to the good, rest assured that there isn't the slightest cause for regret."

12. See *infra,* letter 1, note 6. Fuller details may be found in Manuel Ossa, S.J., "Blondel et Rousselot: Points de vue sur l'acte de foi," in *Mémorial Pierre Rousselot, 1878–1915,* in *Recherches de science religieuse,* 1965.

13. Blondel-Valensin, *Correspondance,* t. 3, letter 56, pp. 126–130. See Teilhard, *Science et Christ,* pp. 63–114. Fr. Teilhard wrote to his friend from Paris, October 13, 1925: "Yes, of course, send me Blondel's letter. *Thank you* for what you've done for me, both of you. And as a start, do convey my thanks to him."

14. Recounted in a letter to Mgr. Bruno de Solages, rector of

the Institut Catholique in Toulouse. Blondel thanked Mgr. de Solages for the talk he delivered on November 18, 1947 (at the official meeting for the reconvening of the Institut). His subject was "Evolution and Its Meaning for Christian Thought" (*Bulletin de littérature ecclésiastique,* October–December, 1947). This talk defended (and quite effectively) Fr. Teilhard against the attacks of several theologians.

We note that Valensin was in the habit of recommending Lachelier's work to his friends (and students)—for its concern with the formal nature of things, their constitutive essence as opposed to their material composition. Teilhard, accordingly, was familiar with it, and refers to it in *Man's Place in Nature* (1950): "Have we, we ask, emerged into consciousness, and not only into consciousness but (as Lachelier says) into consciousness of consciousness only to sink back immediately into an even blacker unconsciousness?" (p. 100). In *Origines humaines* (1928), Edouard Leroy too quotes from Lachelier: "An idea, like a world, is born of nothing" (p. 369)—to illustrate the phenomenon of "invention" in biology. A great deal of space in this book is devoted to Teilhard. This same idea of "invention" is developed in *The Phenomenon of Man,* and on page 171 we read that the "threshold of reflection" is a "mutation from zero to everything." This is one of Lachelier's phrases which Valensin was fond of quoting.

15. Two studies of these tests have been published: Manuel Ossa, S.J., "Possession de l'être et abnégation dans la philosophie de Maurice Blondel," in *Revue d'ascétique et de mystique,* no. 152, October–December, 1962 (27 pages); and Christopher F. Mooney, S.J., "Blondel and Teilhard de Chardin," in *Thought,* 37 (1962), p. 543–562. Fr. Mooney is also the author of a theological study of Teilhard de Chardin's Christology, *Teilhard de Chardin and the Mystery of Christ* (New York and London, 1966). Also see P. Henrici, "Blondel und Teilhard de Chardin," in *Orientierung* (1962). p. 179; M. Barthélemy-Madaule, *Bergson et Teilhard de Chardin* (Paris, 1963), pp. 454–459. There is also an interesting article entitled "De Blondel à Teilhard,

nature et intériorité," by Christian d'Armagnac, S.J., in *Archives de philosophie,* April–June, 1958, pp. 298–312.

In the notes which follow, references to Fr. Teilhard's texts published in the volume *Ecrits du temps de la guerre, 1916–1919* (Paris, 1965) will be indicated merely by the first word in the title, *Ecrits.* A number of references will also be made to our own two works, *La Pensée religieuse du Père Pierre Teilhard de Chardin* (Paris, 1962; = *Pensée religieuse*), and *Teilhard de Chardin, the Man and His Meaning* (New York and London, 1965). As the reader is no doubt aware, the letters which make up the volume *The Making of a Mind* were all written to Teilhard's cousin, Mlle Marguerite Teillard-Chambon.

16. The commentary was conceived with a threefold purpose: (1) to throw light on the vocabulary by pointing out numerous passages in a similar vein; these passages are not drawn from his spiritual and largely contemporaneous writings alone, but from the entire body of his work, (and of course we will sometimes widen the context still further, to pin down certain nuances of thought); (2) to reëstablish the objective meaning of certain texts which have sometimes been subject to serious misinterpretation; (3) to provide students of the Teilhardian work with a certain amount of information which might be of value as bibliography or prove otherwise useful.

1.

Maurice Blondel
to Auguste Valensin

Aix, 5 December 1919

Reverend Father and dear friend,

Here, to comply with your wishes at last, are a number of "reflections"—hardly worthy of the name—on these pages which you were kind enough to have me read. I thank you and ask you to please consider whether it would be worth-while passing them along to your friend. And if you decide that it would, do ask him to forgive me for the free and easy way I have pressed forward into the matter; it is only *brevitatis causa* that I become assertive when, in fact particularly when, I am not on sure ground; to me it seems rash to anticipate the final Revelation by trying to divine what lies behind the veil; when the time comes we will step *exumbris et imaginibus*[1] and *immutabimur*—; still, it is good to maintain that these shadows and images contain a reality in which our eternity is decided, and that the *corpus spiritale*[2] (what a mysterious word) will remain a *corpus*! Nor would I want Fr. Teilhard to feel that I don't value him at his worth. I am raising this note of caution for my own benefit, and have a great deal to learn from him. He is so acute in sensing the infinite distance present in the most intimate of physical contacts, so good at expressing how physical communion and assimilation are only possible within an ascetic and mystic configuration. But all of us have to constantly bear in mind that the assimilating effusion which stems from divine benevolence can only operate and triumph within us at a heavy price and through an excruciating expansion. It is always the mystery of the *Verbum caro factum* and the *caro verbum facta*. The one is only possible through the other.[3] The world is unquestionably divinized; we should go on pilgrimage to the holy places wherever we can. We breathe the air He breathed, and something of Him is circulating within us. But if all this is to attain its full meaning and potency, it must go hand in hand with a vocation for the supernatural, with grace offered and received, lacking which all the divine force entering a creature does him no good (*caro nihil proficit*),[4] in fact is endebting and restrictive, "drained of its goodness" and damning[5] [. . .].

Recherches de science religieuse has just now reached me and of course I looked through it right away for your note. It's wonderful! And how fine it would be if Fr. Rousselot's articles and works could be collected and published—with a commentary by you![6] [. . .]

2.

Maurice Blondel's First Paper to Auguste Valensin

I am stirred with admiration and sympathy for the various essays you sent me. They are most interesting. You would have me note down a few of my impressions. And although I comply, I do so with considerable diffidence, a diffidence which is only increased by my having found there (along with a strong sense of poetry and of the work's achievement of its aims) a few of the oldest and most esoteric themes of my private thought and what you call my "pan-Christism."[1] So perhaps it will be useful to indicate where I am in agreement with the author and where my thinking has developed a little differently from his own.

First, as regards the critical section, I find that my earliest thoughts as a boy and my outlook today correspond almost exactly with his. The generally held notion, even the scientific notion of the body (like the notion of matter) is extremely deficient—the action of our presence is virtually boundless; we act *in toto* as we undergo, direct and make specific within ourselves the action of the Whole.[2] Therefore there is not simply a "universal interdependence" (although my saying so will offend Father de Tonquedec),[3] but an interpenetration; we are literally made up of one another, without ceasing to be this *ineffable individuum,* this ω, which justifies the "myself alone and God alone" of Newman. It is precisely the feeling of this double reality, the singular and the universal, which led me to study

Action, simultaneously the expression of a being's incommunicable originality and a factor within the Whole. This is the very question I raised in the first draft of the thesis I planned back in 1892 and which I still have in my possession. Moreover, with that (and perhaps even prior to all other philosophical questions) the problem of the Incarnation seemed to me to be the touchstone of a true cosmology, a metaphysics complete within itself. Hence the choice of subject for my Latin thesis, *De vinculo substantiali*[4]—a choice made in 1880, quite early, about the time I graduated from the *lycée* and entered Dijon University where M. Joly was making a study of Leibniz. This thesis deals with the problem of how matter "achieves substance" by examining how the unity of the compound (which matter is) can attain corporeality; furthermore, the question raised by Leibniz and des Bosses concerning transubstantiation during the Eucharist leads us to conceive of Christ, without detriment to the constituent monads, as the bond which makes substantiation possible, the vivifying agent for all of creation: *vinculum perfectionis*.[5]

I also share to the letter (and have always shared) the thoughts and feelings of Fr. Teilhard with regard to the problem of the nature of Christ. Our world has expanded through the social and natural sciences. One cannot remain true to Catholicism and be content with a mediocre explanation, a limited outlook which represents Christ as an accident of history, isolating Him in the Cosmos as if He were an episode without proper time and place. One cannot represent Him as an intruder, an alien in the crushing and hostile immensity of the universe. Well before the "Loisyism" of the little red books[6] I was clearly and profoundly aware of the options at hand: either to fall back into a murderous symbolism, or go forward towards a realism which is self-consistent throughout, towards a total reality which puts the metaphysics of Christianity in accord with the mystical theology lived by the saints and even by the faithful following. Having always been a *maximist*[7] I was deeply gratified to see the efforts of the *minimists* rebuffed. The parting of the ways has been reached, and we are led to the *instauratio tota in Christo: de Christo nunquam satis.*

23

So let us go forward without hesitation; as man finds himself and the world expanding before him, we should take a deeper sense of Christ into our eyes and hearts.[8]

Yes—but it is extremely important not to achieve this growth through an excessive reliance upon sense and understanding, as though our scientific knowledge and our rational methods might stand on an equal footing with truths which are properly spiritual and religious in nature. For a long time, I confess, I was too desirous of attaching myself to all phenomena; I bestowed a privileged and almost exclusive and exhaustive character upon our anthropomorphic mode of thought, and cast what we naturally love and our present states as absolutes. But by critical reflection, by the very development of sciences which are less and less anthropomorphic, above all through reading the mystics (the great realists among men),[9] and in undergoing the trials of life, I am increasingly wary of an excessively naturalistic, an excessively physical manner of formulating my concept of the universal function of Christ.[10] I am going to try to explain myself a little more clearly on this point, for it seems to me that the temptations which I had and still have to watch for are very much like those facing Father Teilhard.

I agree that Christ is an incarnate presence in everything, a real presence, and that He is a histological element, if one may say so, in the natural order. But there are two pitfalls to avoid here.

(1) A conceptual picture which we make up through sense impressions or scientific and rational ideas should not be regarded as an even minimally adequate representation of this presence and this role. Doubtless what we perceive and conceive of the real Whole has truth to it. But it is infinitely small in the immensity of the real relationships within the Whole. We should avoid constructing an explaining principle out of what we are drawn to by our cast of mind as scientists—the anthropomorphic mode of thought.[11]

(2) There is a still greater danger we ought to watch out for and that is to suppose (without our even being aware of doing so) that the natural order has a divine stability as natural order,

and that Christ in a physical sense plays the role which pantheism or monism ascribe to their vague and diffuse God. Here we have the overtones of *naturism,* of *hylozoism,* or more accurately of *hylotheism,* whose strangeness will come to light as we follow its formula to its logical outcome; one would have to admit that Christ could be incarnated for reasons other than supernaturalization and that the world, even in the physical sense, were divinized without being supernaturalized—as if God were principally a demiurge on the one hand and on the other were actually physically capable, being what He is, of drawing himself in as participant—and this, while He remained "within the structure," without the supernaturalization which necessarily leads to the *denuo nasci* of spiritual life and grace, with all that follows in the way of moral, ascetic, and mystic transformation. A purely physical supernaturalism makes no sense whatever.[12]

One should also take pains to avoid the luxury of symbols, images and specious conceptions; the more accurate, the more revealing they are in appearance, the more deficient and misleading they are in actuality. True pan-Christism sharply disassociates itself from anything having to do with physicism and pantheism. This means that it is important not to be a "visionary," and the real seer[13] is one who, contemplating in darkness, has the sense of the infinite richness of the mystery, one who never stops, as required by the masters of the mystical life, even at visions which are truly supernatural in character—less still, at symbols of his own invention.

However, one might object, is there not a positive truth in what science and our senses tell us, an aspect and possibly even an element of the Real? Is it not actually a privileged aspect, since our destiny is decided under this species? Doubtless it is, but only one aspect among countless others; it is less meaningful to us, therefore, for the amount of real truth it contains than for the moral decisions, even the sacrifices, it leads us to make. On the one hand, the only real way to avoid becoming unduly specific is to detach oneself from the illusory realism of the intellect and the senses. On the other hand, we should remember that we do not have to conquer the universe, or to find Christ in nature.[14] We have to give up the whole of Creation for the precious Pearl, to die in the world to be nourished by a new life. Hence the dark night which the soul must cross, without a smooth transit from matter to spirit, from the physical to the hypermetaphysical Christ. Fr. Teilhard seems to think we can enter into communion with the Whole (including Christ) without first limiting ourselves to communion with the One, the Transcendent, the Word incarnate, in His concrete and singular human form; with this, as I see it, he is veering away from the truly beautiful and profound thought that inspires him. The test, renunciation, and abnegation are not necessary for the sake of penitence alone; they are essential in light of man's (and through man, the universe's) destiny to attain deification. There is no pessimism, no disdain for matter or sensibility in this return to the conditions which seem onerous to life and to its taking hold; far from it, for love is the foundation and the goal of everything—"*ut vitam abundantius habeani.*"[15] When St. John of the Cross, for example, bids us cross the dark night, it is not a matter of his scorning physical reality, of his failing to appreciate aesthetic beauty or of his denying the needs of the heart; quite to the contrary, he wants to first extricate us from all sensualism, all rationalism, all physicism, in short, rid us of the various forms of anthropomorphic egoism. For abnegation alone, he says, enjoys, possesses, and knows everything through a de-centration and a transfer of the self over to God, such that one feels himself, in the elevated state of union, in divine contact with everything, but beyond the images and concepts which are, and always will be, too anthropocentric in character.[16]

In brief, like Fr. Teilhard, I believe that the time has come for deeper commitment to the doctrine of Emmanuel: "*Testis verus et fidelis,*" "*Alpha et Omega,*" "*in quo omnia constant,*" "*princeps omnis creaturae.*"[17] But one should be on guard against the dangers of immanentism; the more one represents Christ as an innate presence in souls and in the world itself, the more vital it is to lay sharp stress on the absolute transcendence

26

of the divine Gift, on the inescapably supernatural character of the plan towards deification, and thus on the moral transformation[18] and the spiritual expansion which are demanded by and achieved through grace. Although in one sense there is continuity in the universal order, in another sense there is incommensurability, a doing away with[19] the old man and the old nature for the birth of the *"novum coelum"* and the *"nova terra."*[20] It is improper, therefore, to proceed from a scientific outlook and to postulate sense impressions or rational concepts as explaining principles. These symbols are infinitesimally true; they could become perilous or false if this inadequate physicism became enamored of itself to the point of relegating the ascetic and mystical transubstantiation to another plane (a higher plane, be it said)—this transubstantiation which is the only way to prepare the cosmologic integration of Christ.

3.

Pierre Teilhard de Chardin to Auguste Valensin

December 8, 1919

Dear friend,
P. C.[1]

I have just received your correspondence of the 6th. I shall reply in a few days, after thinking about it. But I want to let you know right away that I received it and to tell you how moved I was by what these "green pages" contain. Thank you for putting me in contact with such an elevated thinker, with such a beautiful soul. —Of course I shall send them back to you, along with my thoughts, no doubt asking you to refer them along to him.

This is how I see it at first glance. M. Blondel may be judging me on samples of my prose which are particularly "naturistic" in tone and which do not give a complete picture of my position ("Elijah," in particular).[2] —Then too, there is certainly a difference of opinion between us, or should I say a gap. It would be very profitable if we could clarify and reduce this gap. The "green pages" raise a note of caution; they point to pitfalls which I made clear to myself some time ago—yet never so explicitly—in any case never with the same sharpness of relief which a second, understanding mind gives to things. I shall try to "assimilate" this warning. —You told me that M.

Blondel feels he has gone through the phase where I am now. For the present, I believe I could say the same of him (though I by no means contest his greater insight and experience). As I said in the annotation to my first "paper,"[3] there is communion with the earth (1st phase), communion with God (2nd phase), and communion with God through earth (3rd phase),[4] which hardly excludes the journey through "the night" but rather introduces and justifies it. And here again we find the mysterious notion of "transformation" stepping in; it does not do away with the "critical points"[5] but enables them to fulfill their function—linking super-nature and nature as it does spirit and matter—enabling us to pursue the higher realities *through* the mean husk of all forms, all physical possession . . .[6]

I must try to draw this together and make it clear—then I shall send it to you.

Until then, my deepest thanks and fullest trust, *in Xsto.*

4.

Teilhard de Chardin's First Paper to Auguste Valensin

Paris, December 12, 1919

Dear friend,

Here are the notes which you sent me. I was touched by them, as I told you in my last letter, and read them with real respect. Thoughts such as these, I feel, would serve me to good effect, should I ever find myself in particularly pressing need of correction. So please tell Maurice Blondel how grateful I am for his kindness and his interest in my work. And if you think it would be a good idea, send him this paper I wrote after thinking about his observations.

—To begin with, we agree completely on two essential points:

    A. First (and this is clearly spelled out on both sides) on the fact that Christ should be loved as a world,[1] or rather as *the* world, that is, as the physical center (from which everything is ultimately determined and derives its real substance) imposed on every aspect of the Creation which is destined to survive.[2]

    B. But then too (and this was less clear from the notes you showed him, though I have expressed it elsewhere a number of times) that renunciation and asceticism play a final, all-important role in the construction of the new universe (and are by no means "necessary for the sake of penitence alone"). I am in fundamental agreement with him that the completion of the world is only consummated through a death,[3] a "night", a reversal, an ex-centration, and a quasi-depersonalization of the monads.[4] A monad's integration into Christ presupposes that it has effected a kind of internal disintegration, that is, a modification of its entire being, a requisite to its re-creation and entry into the Pleroma. In essence, union with Christ presupposes that we transpose the ultimate center of our existence into Him—which implies the radical sacrifice of egoism.[5] Granting this, *how* should one visualize ascetic death, the mystic night, Christian renunciation?[6] What is their structure and how do they work? It seems to me that Maurice Blondel and I differ in something on this point (a very significant one for practical purposes, but philosophically of only secondary importance). We ought to try to pin this something down. In an attempt to do so, I am going to restate my present position as clearly as I can. With this formula Maurice Blondel will have a clearer picture of the direction in which I can, or even ought, in this opinion, to modify my attitude.

The first form of *renunciation* which comes to mind is that of a *cutting off,* a *rupture* with the world, an *evacuation,* pure and simple, of the old man. St. John of the Cross,[7] read literally, seems to conceive of the *night* in just this way. Do you want to find God? Close the channels which admit the false, exterior life. When you have done so, "*ipso facto*" the higher light will shine deep within you. The true light will appear as the other vanishes. The noise from outside ceases and you will hear the other voice in your heart. For there are *two* quite distinct lights illuminating you. There are two different words echoing continuously within you. To hear one properly, you must quell the other.[8] —The new earth is a neo-formation[9] (as zoölogists say) which will follow the old earth, pushing it aside and taking its place.

A priori I have no objection, either in mind or heart, to this first manner of visualizing the establishment of the Reign of God. As long as I can regard Christ as a world, as the only definitive world, then I am not greatly concerned whether His omnipresent action on me should have the character of a break, an extinction of the visible world—on the contrary, as I shall explain further on, a transformation.[10]

But here is what I have against the form of renunciation described above—its not being viable to humanity as a whole —thus, its not offering a general solution to the problem of our stance in the face of the supernatural—its not even affording us the maximum possible union with Christ here on earth.[11]

Let me explain.

Everyone finds that an enormous and necessary part of his life is set aside for positive activity, for *human* effort directed to material and social ends.[12] This effort is forced upon us by external circumstances, as sufferance. But it also has a spiritualizing value of prime importance, not only for the moral "training" it gives our activity, *but also* for the positive results accruing from the *work itself*.[13] Who can say how much our mystical life, our most supernatural life, owes to Plato, Leibniz, Pascal, Newton, and to countless (and far less obvious) others whom any one of us could name in his heart? Who would dare gauge the wealth of natural, readily supernaturalizable powers the human soul is still capable of acquiring (as, for example, the soul grows increasingly aware of its integral part in the universe and of the still unexplored spiritual regions promised to the "unanimity" of spirits)? —Who could maintain that charity would not wither if it were cut off from the human sap and struggle, relegated accordingly to a world transformed into a monastery?[14]

In the course of every person's life, in the history of the human race as a whole, there is an enormous store of positive achievement which we cannot, without disloyalty, allow to come to nothing. If Christ is to take on the same dimension as my life—of my life in its *entirety*—it is essential that I feel myself growing in Him, not only through ascetic constraints and the supremely unifying amputations of suffering, but also through everything my existence brings with it in the way of positive effort and the perfecting of my nature and of human duty.[15] —This is necessary; —without it, Christianity *deprives* me of the will to act, and I am left with disgust for one entire side of my life, a side which religion has plucked of its flowers but which it has not given me the right to let fall to the ground.

The formula for renunciation, if it is to be total, must satisfy two conditions:

1. It must enable us to go beyond everything there is in the world.
2. And yet at the same time compel us to press forward (with conviction and passion—because it is a question of life or death) to the development of this same world.[16]

How can this be done?

I think that detachment and attachment, these two properties which are contradictory in appearance and which make up the complete Christian attitude,[17] harmonize quite easily, provided one agrees that the supernatural Pleroma grows out of the natural universe according to a law of transformation, not one of rupture. —Transformation, in that the supernatural actually rearranges the elements of this world, to the point of making them truly *more* and *other than they were*—but also transformation in the sense that the natural elements are absolutely necessary to this work of salvation, providing it with its fuel and with a suitable material. The supernatural fullness of Christ depends upon the natural fullness of the world.[18]

Let us think back to the analogy of the cone, (specifically, of a cone of two nappes). Only by inverting itself, only by reducing its volume to a mere point can the lower nappe pass into the upper. And yet everything that was in the lower has entered the upper, and the upper would not exist if the lower had not flowed into it. Just as spirit appeared in man by making some sort of use of the rudimentary forms of instinct, the supernatural is continuously being formed by the super-creation of our nature.[19]

"We do not have to conquer the universe, or to find Christ in nature. We have to give up the whole of Creation for the precious Pearl." I cannot subscribe *simpliciter* to this view because I find it inapplicable to real life (and to the practices which the Church has come to accept).[20] At certain moments I too groan at the unwieldiness of things. I feel that I would like nothing better than to be assured that I could really *let everything go*—the accumulation of facts, the agitation of ideas, the tumult of societies . . . However, in good faith and despite certain passages in the Gospel, I cannot believe that Our Lord has given us permission to give up our struggle with the natural order. We have no indication that the spiritual power of nature is spent (far from it!) so that we might rightfully devote ourselves to the ascetic effort alone. I think that giving in to this desire to "retreat" would lead to illusion and to a decrease in effort, and that we would soon be punished for it by a cooling off of charity (which lives *etiam* on sustained human passion).[21]

True, our life dream is "the elevated state of union in which one feels himself *beyond images and concepts,* in divine contact with everything. But I believe that here on earth, while we certainly do know the joy of sensing the One Necessary Thing[22] at the heart of everything, we attain it (in success *or* lack of success) only to the degree to which we compel ourselves to determine, through great effort, the specific qualities of the images, concepts and *things*. Speaking in general, Christ gives Himself to us through the world which is to be consummated (*etiam naturaliter*) in relation to Him.[23]

Note the following point carefully: I do not attribute a definitive or absolute value to the various constructions which man is led to establish through his struggle with the natural order. I believe they will disappear, recast into a totally new, unimaginable plane of existence.[24] But I hold that they play a provisional and essential role—being irreplaceable, unavoidable *phases* we must go through (we or the race) in the course of our metamorphosis. What I like about them is not their particular form, but their function, which is to build up mysteriously, first what can be divinized, and then, through the grace of Christ coming down on our endeavor, what is divine.[25]

To sum up, the *complete* Christian endeavor consists, in my opinion, in these three things:

1. In collaborating passionately in the human effort in the conviction that, not only through faithful obedience,[26] but also through the *work* accomplished, we are working towards the completion of Christ, by preparing the material, more or less close at hand, of the Pleroma.[27]

2. In the course of this hard labor, and in the pursuit of an ever widening ideal, achieving a preliminary form of renunciation and of victory over a narrow and lazy egoism.

3. Cherishing the "emptinesses" as well as the "fullnesses" of life—that is, its passivities and the providential diminishments[28] through which Christ transforms directly and eminently into Himself the elements and the personality which we have sought to develop for Him.

All of human activity (all the suffering and all the effort we make, and in this effort, all the *opus* with all the *operatio*)[29] is thus animated and "made specific" by Christ, without any of it being lost. "*Omnia convertuntur in Christum.*" Despite our attachment to things, we detach ourselves from them; and in one sense, our very attachment detaches us, for nature, seen in its true light, possesses a logic, a power of renunciation, of expansion, and of creative death (itself, the first step in the renunciation which Christ organically imposes on his supernatural organs).

In this way detachment and human effort harmonize. And of course the ways in which they can be combined are infinitely varied. There is an infinity of vocations, and an infinity of phases in every life. Within the Church St. Thomas Aquinas and St. Vincent de Paul stand side by side with St. John of the Cross.[30] For each of us there is a time of growth and a time for diminishment. Now constructive human effort is dominant, now mystic annihilation.[31] The important thing to note in these different forms of sainthood is that they are gradations along a single spectrum. All these attitudes spring from the same inner orientation, from a single law which combines the two-fold movement of the natural personalization of man with his supernatural depersonalization *in Christo.*[32]

These thoughts on the renunciation *which transforms* specify the sense in which I feel I can take Christ to be the center of the universe, *even the center of what are considered "natural" areas.*[33] I do not ascribe any sort of "divine stability" to the natural order. Rather, I would say that this order is characterized by a pronounced instability *in Christum,* everything being on a forward tilt[34] inclined towards the *present* center of the Pleroma.[35] It is actually by dint of this forward tilt that Christ has *something* of a demiurge about Him. If the new Cosmos is not to be, in fact, a creation *adjacent to* the old, but will stem from a transformation of our order of things—if, moreover, our *present* universe is to be, in fact, supernaturalized in everything it is (in other words, to have its direction and center *in Christo* alone), then it follows *ipso facto* that Our Lord has the role, physically, of establishing the world at all its levels. Christ is incarnated *solely* for our supernaturalization; but this itself constrains Him to support and complete the natural strata at one and the same time (in somewhat the way the rational soul, as taught by Scholasticism, takes the place of lower substantial forms). And this makes His action on us all the more inevitable, close at hand, and enveloping.[36]

As I write these lines I ask myself whether I am not storming an open door, whether Maurice Blondel will not say, "But I believe that too." For while we may differ in our *leanings,* or at least in what we tend to *stress,* our differences probably do not amount to much more than that—he emphasizing the transcendence of the universal Christ; I, His "physicalness." These attitudes ought to complement one another. To draw them together, let me say that I too believe that the consummation, the *center of gravity* of our universe lies on the side of the transcendent.[37] As the body of Christ grows towards completion, the amount of "spirit" still diffuse in the world tends proportionately towards zero. Research areas shrink up and vanish. The forms of love disappear and are not encouraged.[38] Finally, everything will be ineffably transformed on the other side.[39] It is not inconceivable that a phase of this metamorphosis should take place here on earth. The day may come when the surface of the earth is under total cultivation or has become uninhabitable, and humanity's sole concern (the concern of the species as a whole, and no longer of a select few or "specialists") will be to withdraw more directly and deeply into God in the heart of the mystic night. This is possible. I do not see that the moment has yet come. Laborers are still needed to sustain those at their orisons—and one must be able to explain to them that they are working in Christ, *even in tilling the soil.*[40]

Goodbye. Again, do as you like with this paper. Keep it or send it along, whichever seems best to you.

Faithfully yours *in Christo.*

5.

Maurice Blondel
to Auguste Valensin

Aix, 19 December 1919

Here are my comments* to the pages which you were kind enough to send me. I appreciate Fr. Teilhard's gracious manner and his receptivity to my earlier remarks. His reply is very instructive and it is a real joy for me to find that he has a sense of total realism, of reintegration, and of the sanctification of the universe as it undergoes divinization *per gradus debitos.* This sense of realism is rare among the Catholics, and is rarely sustained with the motivation and justification he brings to bear. For a long time, as you yourself know, I have tried, indeed have always tried, to solve this problem: how to bestow a definitive solidity upon this poor semblance of being which we, and which objects, are; how to make the relative absolute; how to grasp that all this might be worthwhile for the sake of God. And in studying the conditions necessary for this "solidification" of the creature (a term borrowed from St. Augustine, *Confessions,* vol. XI, c. XXX),[1] I found that the logical, metaphysical, moral, and religious avenues of my thought led to this ontogenetic and phylogenetic Pan-Christism which we have so often discussed together.[2] But it is important to be on one's guard against a persistent tendency to fall back into a sort of physi-

cism or anthropomorphism, important not to confuse the substantial product of this divine reintegration with the transitory
modes of the present trial or with the figurative images which
we may picture for ourselves at this stage of things. I wonder
whether Fr. Teilhard does not slightly simplify and alter the
thought of St. John of the Cross.[3] True, this world is not a stage
set, a phantasmagoria which one must recognize as illusion and
flee; to my mind, however, the great mystics have never maintained any such thing; as for the mystical states of St. Theresa,
for example (discussed by the French Philosophical Society),
I made the point that one of the criteria of true mysticity lies
in whether one grows on several fronts at once, not just in love,
but in the practical side of one's nature, in thoughtful far-
sightedness, in the ability to take effective action.[4] The *night*
which St. John of the Cross commends to us is not a suppression or annihilation of reality, even a sensible reality (for
things have their existence in darkness); it is an anticipation
of the dawn which will return us our faculty of seeing, showing
us all the beings which we could not judge or appreciate with
our present means of perception.[5] I think we agree as to the
solution, in and of itself, to these problems. But when it comes
to formulating this solution at this point along the way, and to
defining the means at hand for doing so, we may still differ
in several questions of shading or choice of expression. The
Father seems less concerned than I with stressing the incommensurability of the divine, with pointing out that divinization
is perforce impossible without supernaturalization and that
supernaturalization is impossible without a death and spiritual
rebirth. And if I infuse the supernatural into the depths of our
reality, I do so for this reason—in its transcendent purity it is
perfectly "inconfusible"[6] with the natural order, whatever we
may say about its being immanent in our world; it will not
admit of being naturalized. It is wonderful and quite proper
to join Fr. Teilhard in maintaining that our task, here in this
world and along with this world, is to construct the divinizable;
but finally the divinizable is not divinized without the spiritual
ferment of mystic immolation, however rudimentary its form in

certain people. In brief, the method of divinization which he outlines for practical purposes, and which he asks us to consider here in the abstract, does not, I fear, reply to St. Augustine's *"distentus per omnia"* (*Conf.* XI, XXIX) which prescribes that one start by being *"purgatus et liquidus igne amoris"* before one is and in order that one be *"extentus et intentus per omnia in omnibus."* For *"forma* mea, *veritas* Tua, *Domine"*.[7]

Again, my apologies, and my very best wishes, . . .

* They are quite jumbled due to my present state of fatigue, and I am hesitant about sending them to you. But for the time being I cannot redo them as I should. Do forgive me.

6.

Maurice Blondel's Second Paper to Auguste Valensin

19 December 1919

I would like to ask you to convey my sincere thanks to Fr. Teilhard. I am grateful to him for his cordiality and his receptivity to my improvised remarks; indeed they were unjustified at times. I also want to apologize for my rash judgements or for my taking him to task for ideas I merely inferred from his work. At heart these were nothing but hypothetical arguments. I am pleased to find us in closer agreement than I thought possible, and on points which were not raised in the beginning but which came to light in the course of our discussion. Finally, I want to reassure him as to my own nature; I am hardly as acosmic or troglodytic as he seems to fear, nor is it my good fortune, believe me, to live "in a monastery."

This apprehension of his seems to result from an extension or shifting of the problem we originally raised; the question (at least as I understood it) was one of establishing, through a sort of theoretical anticipation of the final Revelation, the nature of the process, *"in se, nondum quoad nos,"* by which the creation is totally reintegrated *"in Christo, per Christum, in Deum et in Deo"* and how we might legitimately go about forming a picture *"in via"* of something of this absolute truth, the union *"in*

41

termino".[1] Now then, this is where we started, but Fr. Teilhard raised what seems to me a different question, in any case, one which I had not intended to reply to in his terms; and the question is this: what is the value, from a practical and moral point of view, of this world we live in—of science, philosophy, art, civilization, and human endeavor; it is true, is it not, that this viaticum already constitutes a communion, a deification, in a physical sense, even when the forms it takes are anonymous and natural in appearance? But it is another matter, to my way of thinking, to project onself into the final outcome as it were, and into the absolute, so that one might explain the entire journey "*sub specie aeternitatis*"; another matter to take the position of the traveler and to adopt our present view of things as one considers "the enormous and necessary part of life reserved for human effort, directed to material and social ends." For it is true, this positive effort can be the vehicle of a reality which, though it does become immanent everywhere, is no less transcendent, consuming, and transforming for doing so. To my mind, these are two quite separate problems, and if Fr. Teilhard had wanted to handle them as one from the beginning, then I am guilty of an *ignoratio elenchi* and must make amends in my own way, giving them each a separate answer. The solutions differ, and this is why I still cannot help but feel that the questions should be treated separately, even if one maintains, as I am going to try to do, that as we conceptualize our supernatural destiny and reality, the more we resist "physical" images and natural thought-pictures, the more seriously we take our duties here on earth and the more importance we attach to human effort under the species in which it appears, spontaneously, in each of our lives, and in the history of civilization in general.

(1) —As for the question he raised on thinking critically about my notes, I am very happy to have his encouragement and support as I continue along a road which I took despite grave misgivings, where I am drawn by a desire which is central to Fr. Teilhard's life too, namely the desire not to sanction absenteeism and idleness, not to allow the Pleroma to lose anything of its richness, not to see opposites in God the Re-

deemer and God the Architect and Creator, the desire to keep loving watch over all forms of life and of being by taking all the stammerings of thought and all the poor phenomena from which we have drawn something of our sustenance and into which we have put something of our heart and integrating them all back into the absolute; the desire to consummate the total unity of the Creature in divine oneness and charity.[2] This is a road where one feels a glimmer of the loving cheer of St. Francis of Assisi.[3] But as I made my fervent way along it, I was nevertheless held back, troubled for long periods by all the testimonies and authorities who advised against it. It almost seemed as if Catholicism were going against the grain of this embracing, expanding doctrine, to aim at the elimination and censure of any attachment to this world, *"totus in maligne positus"*; the uneducated and journalists (such as those whose opinions I gathered for *L'Univers, La Verité* or *La Croix*) are not the only folk to maintain that science is dangerous and bad, that our civilization is both corrupt and corrupting from top to bottom; there are theologians (publishing in the *Revue thomiste* and elsewhere) and Christian sociologists like Le Play who believe that the only thing that matters is personal sanctification and that the entire movement of humanity, the aspect of this world as a whole, anything beyond observing the eternal Ten Commandments, is vanity, affliction of the spirit, perversion of the heart.[4] But it does not stop here. The general current in the Church runs counter to the "growth" of humanity, does it not?—counter to social and scientific progress, counter to a Christian philosophy of history which would see a providential meaning in phylogenesis; as though all our knowledge stemmed, in fact, from the Fall (this, literally, is what has been said), and as though the state of atonement might be won by returning to the innocence of the simple, the detachment of the ignorant who have fled "worldly life." Now I have never been able to come to terms with this particular outlook, nor to believe that phylogeny, like the ontology of every Christian, might not be destined for supernaturalization. Fr. Teilhard's doctrine is so clear and strong on this point. Again, I must say how encouraged I am by it, how much confidence and reassurance it has given me.[5] Therefore, we do not disagree on fundamentals, but there is a certain *malentendu* between us, or should I say a difference of opinion as to the mode by which the phylogenic development of the whole world is to be supernaturalized, a difference in our respective ways of picturing the passage "from the divinizable to the divine" or rather, from the divinizable to the divinized.

(2) —It seems to me that we agree as to the toll to be paid for individual entry into supernatural life. We also see eye to eye on the onerously salutary, onerously loving necessity of the *"denuo nasci."* To live in God, one must allow the egoism of the old, the former, man to perish, and open oneself to the expanding, crucifying entry of a God who does not stoop down to our size, who would have us grow up to His, an increase beyond anything we could imagine had we not had the Revelation.[6] But this is where we ought not to confuse separate problems. One must draw a distinction between detachment which effects supernaturalization (*paupertas spiritu*) and renunciation proper (*rebus*). Still greater care should be taken to distinguish the stimulating aid we can and ought to find in things (as though they were already phylogenically supernaturalized and divinely nourishing) from the ultimate reintegration which these things will one day afford all the elect *"in termino"* or which they already partially afford the saints who have attained the state of mystical marriage. I can hardly feel, therefore, that I underrate the true, good, and solid character of the struggle with the natural order of human effort or of scientific work by considering these endeavors a path providentially assigned to the greater part of the human race and subordinating them to the work of supernatural birth, the condition *sine qua non* of deification for everybody. Quite to the contrary, I praise the grandeur, spirit and beauty of human endeavor, praise it to the highest, this efford to "build the divinizable," a work one should never fear to exalt beyond its due, in order that the holocaust might seem more precious, the cost of the sacrifice the greater. This is the traditional position, is it not?—man's enormous worth, then an immeasurable increase (*haud condignae . . .*)[7] resulting from the combined action of will and of grace. No, "Chris-

tianity should not deprive us of our will to act"; moreover, this spirit should grow as the action itself spreads out beyond strictly human affairs, increasing its scope to become, as it must and ought, the receptacle, the vehicle, the pyre, the host of the divine fire.[8]

But the fire *itself* is not found in "human endeavor"; it is not a physical presence there, nor in humanity, nor in the world *ut sic*. And if I still have two reservations with respect to Fr. Teilhard's system of thought (again unjustified, no doubt), here is how I would put them: he sometimes, it seems to me, in his desire to bring Christ into our effort, into the world transfigured in the eyes of his faith, tries to conceptualize the immanence of the supernatural in terms which are too physical in character; at other times (and this amounts to more than a form of Gnosticism), he phylogenically divinizes the universe through a sort of millenarian ontology, as if this universe, its natural order off balance in a forward tilt, found support and solidification in Christ, this in turn contributing to our own solidification on this plane. This is tantamount to saying that the supernatural is a constituent element of the universe, an element like any of the others, illuminating these others, to be sure, transfiguring them even, but not consuming and transubstantiating them.[9] As I see it, charity is not sustained by human passions *ut sic*[10]; if one gives some thought as to what divine incommensurability means, one realizes that supernaturalization is no simple feat. I find Jansenism repugnant just as I find Humanism sanctimonious, and Christian Science disappointing. It is also important not to supernaturalize the natural and not to naturalize the supernatural either in assertions one might make about them or in one's manner of dealing with them. Those who are closest to the *Passion* are also the most *active* of men, and the most human.[11] Pure detachment binds us firmly to everything; but we do not reach the salutary "emptiness" through the "fullnesses"—not at all. Fullness is to be found in emptiness, as is God and the rest too. The beginnings of fullness should not be sought in an involvement with things.[12]

45

7.

Teilhard de Chardin's Second Paper to Auguste Valensin

Paris, 29 December 1919

Dear friend,

I am returning the "yellow pages" with this letter. When I first acknowledged receiving them, I wrote you that they had been of great value to me. And this is quite so. I was impressed by their clarity of expression, and found that they struck a note of perfect resonance with my own most vital thoughts. As it turns out then, I am rewarded for making an unintentional detour around the original question, for this prompted Maurice Blondel to share with me his "faith" in the value of the human phyletic effort. If I made a detour, I did so instinctively, following my strong tendency to begin searching for the divine where it is for us now—in the form of some element which may be reached (by faith[1] and good will[2]) on all the outer surfaces and in every inner layer of things.

This time, it seems to me, the point in question has been clearly defined by Maurice Blondel: "What can we say about the *mode* by which reality is divinized? What is the process which nature undergoes as it is integrated into the Pleroma?"

I shall try to define my own position and relate it to what I believe to be Maurice Blondel's view of the matter.

To begin with, I wholeheartedly agree that the universal striving of this world can be regarded as *the preparation for a holocaust*.[3] The world, through its spiritual advances (the summation of all other advances), develops in effect a power to adore, which amounts to a capacity to renounce. The world fashions its individual and collective consciousnesses for one purpose—nourishes, refines, and frees them for a single supreme act—for their choice to return to God and to sacrifice their apparent (or immediate) autonomy to Him. If there is anything here which I would call millenarianism,[4] it is the spirit inherent in an age when men have become aware of their unity with *all their fellows,* have realized that they are intimately bound up with all the rest, and have come into possession of the *fullness of their soul* which they may throw freely onto the divine pyre.[5] All our work, finally, goes into making up the host on which the divine fire will descend.

Here we agree.

But what actually happens to a creature when he is "consumed in God"?

Maurice Blondel stresses two images, the *fire which devours* and the *fire which transfigures,* using them to characterize and contrast our respective ways of conceptualizing the divinizing process. I am wondering whether in the reality of things, these two expressions do not amount to the same thing.[6]

How in fact does God "consume" us in beatification?

Not by annihilating us, certainly, so that He may then re-create us. Divine ardor acts, destroys, but leaves something of us in existence.[7] But again, what is this residue left from our advances in the natural order, and hence capable of divinization? Let us reduce it as much as we can and say that the only "molded" element to pass from our natural to our supernatural state is our gift taken as a whole, the sincerity of our self-abnegation, the fullness of our option. Merely by recognizing that our free choice is the flower of our spiritual fullness, we realize that this single germ of ourselves (retained by divine action for forming us anew) would preserve us and would be capable of reproducing us completely, body and soul. *In my act of deciding to give myself over to God, all of me passes into the supernatural,* not just my innermost personality but all the shadings and details of my past. Therefore, if a living option is the element within me to undergo divinization (and "the works which follow us" come down to at least that!), if it is fire which is to recast me, then it is also quite true to say that this fire will consume me and spell my death. In speaking of its flames, one must say that they devour in order to emphasize the unimaginable grandeur of their work of recasting. But one should also add that they preserve us too, to make this point—as our natures undergo sublimation we retain all the elements our human liberty has amassed, the large and the small alike. For Grace, consuming and transfiguring are one and the same process.[8]

In any case, I do feel this strongly. It is vitally important that the sanctifying process be disassociated from anything which might lend it an air of naturalism, humanism, or Christian Emersonianism.[9] This would clear up humiliating (and disastrous) ambiguities as to its nature. A precise formula would serve this purpose. I am hopeful of finding a definition of this transformation which divinizes our being, a definition which would "contradistinguish" this form of transformation, through its very mode of operation, from all others and from all breaks in the natural order (such as those separating matter and life, life and thought). But I wonder whether the very structure of the world does not militate against this attempt. There are other peaks between us and the chasm of the supernatural.[10] The spiritual soul's invasion of the body is already a sort of fire which consumes matter, is it not? When the unbeliever is in the throes of cosmic revelation (see W. James), is he not, on his primitive groping level, already striking the attitude of the chosen who surrenders himself to God and is taken by Him? Is not the supreme lesson of *all* life that death is necessary if we want to live (a lesson so true that Greek humanism ought to be considered an out and out natural heresy)? One prepares for the decisive metamorphosis through a series of moultings which are models of this ultimate change of state, though on a much lower order. There is a sort of continuity in the successive discontinuities which the creature passes through on his way to God. I wonder whether this "graduation" would not prevent us (with mounting opposition) from characterizing this "excessus" of our life into God[11] in a single word—a word which would be applicable to this act alone.

It is quite true that the fire which takes possession of us and recasts us as supernatural beings—whatever its mode of operation—is of *unparalleled* incommensurable power. But God is not utterly beyond reach, even from where we now stand. Through His incarnation, He *made Himself* in some way an *element* of our universe—a superior element, to be sure, a super-element, but one which may be understood *by analogy* with our elements (or with what would constitute a "soul of the world"). *The Fire of heaven* which consumes us, reaches us in (and after) embracing the world; consequently the fire is, in part, the Fire of the earth; and the universe, *born of fire, now* counts fire among its analogical but real constituent parts.[12]

Due to this universal conflagration we are plunged into, it is (blissfully) inevitable, in my opinion, that one go on to say that Christ solidifies *totaliter, etiam naturaliter,* —because solidification of the individual is only realized within the solidification of the whole—and the whole holds together, top to bottom, solely through the final cohesion—and there is but one center—ω, Our Lord Jesus Christ.[13]

Of course this solidification of everything *in Christo* is still *in fieri,* still forthcoming. That is why we can hypothetically stop the flow of time and imagine the world at a stage where it is sustaining itself *naturaliter, extra Christum.* But in reality this break does not exist; each creature has but one *stable* factor of life enveloping it completely, and that is its (more or less imminent) destiny to enter the Pleroma, or to take part in it for a certain length of time. And here is the proof: separation from Christ is enough to spell the corruption (both spiritual and material) of the damned.[14]

I have sometimes thought of modifying this view (its abso-

49

lute character, and its improbability at first glance) by postulating that the world *extra Christum* enjoyed an initial existence *sufficient unto itself.* The only souls to step out of this initial circle and to enter Christ's field of divinization (bringing *their world* with them) would be those whose lives cleave to Christ through faith and good intention. Thus there would be, *a parti rei,* two distinct compartments in the universe: the world which has been created and the world of Christ (the latter gradually absorbing the former). It seemed to me that this modification was illogical—at odds with the identity of God the Creator and Redeemer—incompatible with the rise of the natural order as a whole (so readily evident in the evil of damnation).[15]

In one sense grace does not usher man into another universe.[16] It guides him into a prolongation of our universe where nothing of what we are remains *ut sic* but where every element

—is utilized *ut sic*

—passes through something of itself (—resurrection of the flesh). Everything in the present world (except certain aspirations, a certain leaning toward the divine) maintains its form and natural appearance. But at heart everything is already animated by the divine.[17]

Maurice Blondel objects to my tendency to *"extendere hominem et omnia"* before man has concentrated himself in Christ, thereby running the risk of having us *"distendi per omnia."* I too recognize this danger. But it seems to me that this process is necessary, and that the risk can be *avoided.*[18] It is necessary to extend the will *ad omnia* first, because the Whole has the specific virtue of awakening us to the divine vision. But quite apart from that, if we had to wait for mystical unification with Christ before we addressed ourselves to the world, we would probably never begin our human effort. An extension into things and a concentration *in Christum* are perforce two movements performed simultaneously.[19] As soon as man has had his first mystical awakening, as soon as he has discovered universal convergence, that is, Christ at the heart of everything (probably, all things considered, the very state which Maurice Blondel calls "*purgatus et liquidus in igne amoris*"), he is no longer prone to a dispersion of his energies as he strives to dominate the real; because now the Whole has become One for him, through the "*within*"; moreover, he discovers, without loss to his activity, the secret of spiritual detachment (an attitude much more difficult to explain than real detachment because it seems to be an unmanageable compromise). He who seeks in all things an element which is *forever out of reach in the direction of effort and enlargement,* is one who achieves real self-abnegation and inner coherence.[20] Finally, everything will be possessed in our Lord . . . For the present, there is a search for Our Lord in everything.

True, it is the "emptiness" in ourselves (subsequently filling with God) which is enriching and beatifying. But one should keep these three points in mind:

1. The emptiness (attracting God) can only be hollowed out in the core of a preëxisting fullness.

2. More remains of this fullness than a mere counter-impression (there is assimilation).

3. Finally, while formal logic would have the notion of fullness excluding the notion of emptiness, this is not true of *life.* There are forms of fullness which organically extend into (reach completion in) forms of hollowness, *fullnesses which are the initial form of an emptiness* (such as the main cavities of the organism; these often take the form of solid fullnesses in the embryo, subsequently emptying . . .); *the very logic of man's development,* I believe, leads him to *the desire to enter something greater than himself.* And this is precisely where the "spiritual power" of matter lies.[21] The fruit must be ripe before it can split and open.[22]

I do not know whether these rather burdensome thoughts will make sense to you. Once again I feel that Maurice Blondel and I differ only in what each of us tends to stress, both of us skirting the same truth, one going too far, the other not far enough. I fear that here again I have detoured around the onerous question (of how much "physicalness" the divine Fire has— of the mode by which it transforms) without addressing myself to it directly. Maurice Blondel will excuse me and give me further assistance. But I do hope he understands that I too speak with great hesitation, particularly when it comes to the fine points in which our interpretations differ. I am absolutely convinced that there is infinitely more truth in the empirical, complex attitude of the Church than in all our simplifying philosophies.[23] While the practices of the saints may be difficult to ground in rational terms, they are "imposed" reality, they are concrete truth. It is they, therefore, which should mould our efforts at systematization,[24] and they will always lie beyond reach. Our speculations will remain sterile for us and for others unless we manage to live by them and transform them into examples.[25]

Goodbye—do convey my deep thanks to Maurice Blondel for trying to help me see my way through these problems. Tell him too that I am grateful for the salutary influence which his particular approach (more traditional and "orthodox," finally, than mine) may have on my thoughts in the future.[26]

Faithfully yours in Christ.[27]

NOTES

1.

Maurice Blondel to Auguste Valensin

1. This was an expression adopted by Newman: "*Ex umbris et imaginibus ad veritatem.*" For Teilhard and Newman, see *infra*, p. 84, n. 21.

2. See I Cor. 15, 44–46. "*Immutabimur*": v. 52.

3. See Yves de Montcheuil, S.J., "Le 'Vinculum' leibnizien d'après M. Blondel," in *Revue apologétique*, February, 1931; *Mélanges théologiques*, Paris, 1951, p. 294: "For him, the humanity of Christ is not a provisional instrument . . . From this point on, everything which is human relates to Christ and shares in the divine . . . If Christ is the prime goal, the highest aim of divine purpose, if in our present world he is the *primogenitus omnis creaturae*, he *in quo omnia constant*, should we, in reading a searching analysis of what we are, be surprised to encounter various expressions of this truth? And could one claim to have given a complete explanation of our universe, its structure, and the drama which is being played out here, if one left out this element which is essential to it?"

4. See Jn. 6, 63: "*Spiritus est, qui vivificat; caro non prodest quidquam.*" Blondel renders the meaning of this passage but only approximates the original wording, as he was wont to do.

5. See Pierre Rousselot, S.J., "Les yeux de la foi", in *Recherches de science religieuse*, t. 1, 1910, pp. 474–475: "*Daemones credunt, et contremiscunt!* As we imagine a mind which has completed its journey and which is fully conscious of its relationship to the final Purpose, we should not conceive of its perceptions as 'free' as are our own, but as permeated

with feeling. The angel or the blessed see God in proportion to the love they bear Him; the fiend is a believer in that, tending towards God with all his nature, he feels his entire person repulsed. The supernatural fills him, but he experiences it drained of its goodness, as we say . . ." In a Note on "La foi des démons" also published in *Recherches* at the end of 1919 (t. 9, pp. 381–382), Fr. Auguste Valensin tried to give a brief explanation of this "apt metaphor": "The fiend . . . does see the lovely, but in the guise of the detestable . . . It is not as though the supernatural did not exist for him . . . Eyes without sight create another form of perception, etc." Fr. Rousselot did not say where he borrowed this term "drained of goodness"; it is consistent with the inner logic of his doctrine, and the idea may have been suggested to him by Maurice Blondel's paper, *Principe élementaire d'une logique de la vie morale* (*Bibliothèque du premier Congrés international de philosophie,* t. 2, Paris 1900; *Premiers Ecrits,* t. 2, pp. 123–147), in which $\eta\tau\tilde{\eta}\sigma\iota\varsigma$ and $\sigma\tau\acute{\epsilon}\rho\eta\sigma\iota\varsigma$ are opposites, the latter not doing away with what it excludes, but retaining it by engendering a privative perception of it. This paper (which Blondel was to reprint in *L'Etre et les êtres,* excursus 23, pp. 467–485, with modifications and clarifications) had made a strong impression on Auguste Valensin; he published a résumé of it in the *Revue de philosophie* (t. 22, 1913, pp. 278–285: *De la logique de l'Action*); in 1925 the censors refused him permission to reproduce the paper in his book *A travers la métaphysique* and he brought it out in the appendix to his translation of *L'Essence de la théorie de la science par Fichte* (*Archives de philosophie,* t. 4, 1926, pp. 126–133: *De la logique de l'Action* d'après M. Maurice Blondel). See Auguste Valensin, *Textes et documents inédits,* p. 168; Blondel-Valensin, *Correspondance,* t. 1 (1957), pp. 271 and 285. A similar idea is expressed in a play by Gabriel Marcel, *Le Chemin de Crête* (1936), in the final scene: "The worst thing about life is that the possessions taken from us are not only missing, but they are in us too, but as unpleasant shadows, like devastating powers of the night" (Ariane the Prior).

6. Several attempts were made to collect the published and unpublished works of Fr. Rousselot (who fell at Eparges, near

Verdun, in the spring of 1915), but the project never materialized. At that time, the papers which he left were all with Fr. Auguste Valensin, in Lyons. Since then, several heretofore unpublished pieces have appeared in the *Recherches de science religieuse* and the *Archives de philosophie* as well as in *Quaestiones de conscientia* (lessons of the Institut Catholique in Paris, 1912; *Museum Lessianum*, sectio theologica, 35, Paris-Brussels, 1937, Preface by Fr. Joseph Huby). A German translation of "Les yeux de la foi" appeared in 1962 in the collection *Christ Heute* (Einsiedeln): *Die Augen des Glaubens* (84 pp.), with a Preface by Joseph Truetsch. For Fr. Pierre Rousselot (1878–1915): Léonce de Grandmaison, S.J., Preface to the reissue of *L'Intellectualisme de saint Thomas d'Acquin* (43 pp). Teilhard speaks of his friend Rousselot in two letters to his cousin, on October 15, 1915, and June 29, 1916 (*The Making of a Mind*). "Alas! where is Rousselot! . . ." he wrote Fr. Victor Fontoynont, on July 22, 1916 (*Pensée religieuse*, p. 352). For Rousselot and Blondel: Blondel-Valensin, *Correspondance, passim*. There are frequent allusions to Rousselot's thought in Blondel's late works: *La Pensée*, t. 2, p. 283, *L'Etre et les êtres*, p. 277; *L'Action*, t. 1, pp. 368 and 430; *La philosophie et l'esprit chrétien*, t. 1, pp. 34 and 264; *Exigences philosophiques du christianisme*, p. 109. On September 24, 1913, Fr. Valensin wrote to Blondel from Paris concerning the article "Intellectualisme" which Rousselot had written for Fr. A. d'Alès' *Dictionnaire apologétique;* the article had been somewhat mutilated by the censors: "Fr. Rousselot has asked me whether you come to Paris from time to time; he would like very much to see you [. . .] I have read his *Intellectualisme,* or at least what is left of it. You would have been pleased with it; I don't think you will be dissatisfied with it. Even when he forms a personal attachment to formulas of a strictly logical intellectualism, it seems to me that he is still extremely close to you." Also see *Valensin, Textes et documents inédits*, p. 77. The third issue of *Recherches de science religieuse* of 1965 is devoted entirely to the work of Fr. Rousselot in honor of the 50th anniversary of his death: *Mémorial Pierre Rousselot.* He had been the first secretary of the magazine.

2.

Maurice Blondel's First Paper
to Auguste Valensin

1. For this "pan-Christism" see the texts collected in Blondel and Valensin, *Correspondance,* t. 1, pp. 43–48. On March 12, 1899, Blondel wrote to Fr. D. Sabatier about Fr. Laberthonnière's *Dogmatisme moral:* "This dogmatism is too narrow in that it restricts itself to moral questions alone. . . . It deals with the practical, the comforting, the empirical side of Emmanuel's role, but not with the metaphysical, the essential, the side which causes things to happen. . . ." (*Lettres philosophiques de Maurice Blondel,* Paris, 1961, pp. 175–176). Abbot J. Wehrlé, July 11, 1904: "The problem of the simultaneity and relationship [within Christ] of a human mode of perception, on the one hand, and of divine knowledge on the other, is connected to, is an aspect of, and is the key to the problem of the coexistence of the infinite Creator with the created, finite world" (in René Marlé, *Au coeur de la crise moderniste,* Paris, 1960, p. 235). Later, Blondel was to become more cautious, or possibly more timorous. To Fr. Laberthonnière, April 26, 1926: ". . . What I called my charitism, my pan-Christism, is in fact the opposite to a 'metaphysics,' even if it were taken to be a metaphysics of charity . . ." (Maurice Blondel and Lucien Laberthonnière, *Correspondance philosophique,* compiled and edited by Claude Tresmontant, Paris, 1961, p. 338). Also see a letter to Fr. Auguste Valensin, December 2, 1930, concerning an article which the latter was writing as a forerunner to the

58

forthcoming publication of *Une énigme historique* (see note 4): "I would advise against your offering your proofreaders and your readers the uncommon and ambiguous term *pan-Christism.* If one is not prepared for it, if there is no explanation of what it means, it may well, by analogy with the word *pantheism,* suggest the idea of a necessary coherence, of a physical or metaphysical continuity, etc."; "For finally, the role of Christ, *in quo omnia constant,* is less ontological, in the abstract sense of the word, than it is spiritualizing through the transforming union, etc."; "You understand my reticence about expressing a truth which is subject to all sorts of confusion and which is therefore very difficult to uphold" (*Correspondance,* t. 3, 1965, pp. 169–170). An earlier letter, May 15, 1929, speaks in the same vein (pp. 156–157). Blondel's vision was "toned down by the *malentendus*" (M. Barthélemy-Madaule, *Bergson et Teilhard de Chardin,* p. 454). See Teilhard, "Mon Univers" (1924): "One can readily see that this 'pan-Christism' has nothing falsely pantheistic about it, etc." (*Science et Christ,* p. 87). "If Christianity is to maintain its place at the forefront of humanity, it must make itself felt as a sort of 'pan-Christism,' which merely comes down to the notion (carried to its conclusion) of the Mystical Body and to one's extending to the universe those attributes which are already recognized (above all, socially) as belonging to Christ the King" (*ibid.,* p. 163). And "Super-Humanité" (1943; *Science et Christ* p. 163). See Jean Mourous, "Maurice Blondel et la conscience du Christ," in *L'Homme devant Dieu,* t. 3 (Paris, 1964), pp. 185–207; in particular pp. 190–192. Henri Bouillard, *Blondel et le christianisme* (Paris, 1961), pp. 160–163; with allusions to the influence of St. Bernard. Jean Rimaud, "Vie spirituelle et philosophie, Maurice Blondel," in *Christus* (1962). Józef Wolinski, "Le Panchristisme de Maurice Blondel," in *Teoresi,* 17 (1962), pp. 97–120. See note 5.

2. See *Journal,* March 14, 1890: "The great hidden truth in evolutionism is this—that the subject is shaped out of its very object, *de limo terrae,* that the world does indeed form a system, like a single animal, that there is not just an ideal plan and a

logical sequence, but an ascending kinship and filiation as well, the same food, the same blood, nature feeding on and rising out of nature, while God is still continually in everything, everywhere, for everything."

3. See Joseph de Tonquédec, S.J., *Immanence, Essai critique sur la doctrine de M. Maurice Blondel,* Paris, 1913; 3rd ed., 1933; Part II, "Philosophical Criticism," Ch. 1, "The Principle of Universal Interdependence" (pp. 59–62), and Ch. 2, "The Value of Knowledge" (pp. 63–115): "The principle of universal interdependence, as applied to knowledge, is one of the traditional arguments of skepticism . . . One could hardly say that M. Blondel has brought something new to the argument. . . . Do I have to work out the position of Sirius to know the form and color of this paper I am writing on?, etc." (pp. 64–66). See t. 3 of the correspondence between Blondel and Valensin for the publication of this book, the controversy surrounding it, and the acute distress it caused Blondel. Scheuer, S.J., of Louvain, published a serious criticism of this work in *Le Vanneur,* a Belgian bibliographic journal: "Here, for example, is one of the most persuasive arguments brought to bear by the author of *Immanence:* 'It will always be true that Duke Henry de Guise was assassinated at Blois in 1588, at the command of the King of France, Henry III. When a schoolboy learns this, he comes into a full and unchallengeable bit of knowledge. One can, then, acquire detailed knowledge without recourse to the lens opening out onto the Whole' (p. 70). Clearly, no increase in knowledge will ever turn the thrust of a dagger into a kiss or an embrace. This is the sort of everyday observation which M. de Tonquédec employs as the middle term of his arguments!, etc."

4. See *Lettres philosophiques de Maurice Blondel,* pp. 9–13: to Emile Boutroux; to the Dean of the Sorbonne. Also see *Une énigme historique, le "Vinculum substantiale" d'après Leibniz et l'ébauche d'un réalisme supérieur* (Bibliothèque des Archives de philosophie, 1930); covering letter to Fr. Auguste Velensin (pp. v–xix). This work is not a mere translation but a recasting of the Latin thesis of 1893. *L'itinéraire philosophique de Maurice Blondel,* p. 57. Jean Brun, "Leibniz et Blondel," in

Hommage à Maurice Blondel, University of Dijon, 27 (1962), pp. 25–37. For the difficulties involved in the writing and publication of the 1930 version, see Blondel-Valensin, *Correspondance,* t. 3 (1965), pp. 144–146 and 151–170.
5. See M. Blondel to J. Wehrlé, May 9, 1904: "Humanity's striving will not be deterred from integrating Christ into a cosmology: otherwise, Jesus would not be the Word." — "It is striking," writes Claude Soucy, "to find how closely Teilhard's mature thought echoes the young Blondel's inquiries into the *vinculum substantiale,* like, for example, the latter's position on *Action*" (*Esprit* [March, 1964], p. 400). On August 8, 1919, Teilhard wrote from Jersey to his cousin Marguerite Teillard: "He [Auguste Valensin] told me that Blondel has such strong ideas on the consistence of the universe *in Christo* that he doesn't dare to go all the way with him—even though, he added, Rousselot didn't hesitate to do so. I wasn't familiar with that side of Blondel's thought and I'm going to try to learn more about it" (*The Making of a Mind,* p. 300). See *Pensée religieuse,* pp. 86–92 and 144–147. Teilhard must have made good use of these explanations Auguste Valensin gave him: "The entire problem of understanding the Mystical Body is linked to the introduction, in philosophy, of the idea of 'the substance of substance' (= larger forms harboring a succession of smaller forms . . .) (note of March 8, 1924). Blondel's idea that "everything holds from above" is developed at great length in "Mon univers" (1924), being used to define and add meaning to Teilhard's own concept of the "creative union." (Compare in particular with "the allegory of the cottage," the excerpt of a letter which Blondel wrote to Fr. Valensin, in *Une énigme historique,* Appendix D, pp. 143–145.) *Science et Christ,* pp. 77–81: "Doubtless certain minds are taken aback by 'the idea of incomplete substances arranged in a hierarchy'; however, all philosophies which lack these two notions of 'incomplete substance' and 'the substance of substance' are cramped and incoherent." In *La pensée,* t. 1, p. 4, Blondel writes that the *vinculum vitale et substantiale,* the *nexus unionis* is the element

which, if not present, "causes everything to break up into fine dust."

The idea that "everything holds together from above" will be developed in a wider context in *The Phenomenon of Man;* p. 43: "If things hold and hold together, it is only by reason of complexity, *from above.*"

6. Alfred Loisy, *L'Evangile et l'Eglise* (1902); *Autour d'un petit livre* (1904), etc. Blondel took an active part in this controversy. See René Marlé, *Au coeur de la crise moderniste.*

7. At times Blondel went so far as to speak of his "integrism" or his "integralism." See his letter to Fr. Auguste Valensin of June 10, 1931: ". . . Whenever I was taken to task for 'minimizing,' in my heart of hearts I replied thus to my attacker: "You think of yourself as a *maximist,* but no; *et plus ego:* it is I who feel that you reduce, that you impoverish and denaturize the Good Tidings; your integrism is merely a poor caricature of my integralism, of my pan-Christism' " (Blondel-Valensin, *Correspondance,* t. 3, pp. 178–179). See *supra,* p. 58, note 1. Here again, Pierre Teilhard's position corresponds with Blondel's: see "L'Elément universel" (Epiphany, 1919), (*infra,* p. 94, note 36); and letter of October 4, 1950 (to M. Gorce): ". . . The stem springing from Rome, *taken in its integrality,* is to me nothing less than the biological structure of sufficient breadth and differentiation to launch and maintain the expected transformation" (in Maxime Gorce, *Le concile et Teilhard,* 1963, p. 198). He spoke of his own "integrism (diametrically opposed to the integrism cited above in Blondel's letter to Valensin)." See St. Augustine, *De vera religione,* c. 5, n. 9: "*Christiani catholici . . . id est integritatis custodes*"; Fr. Joseph Pegon translates these last two words as "*avec leur fidélité entière*" (with all of their fidelity), which brings out the double meaning which the context does seem to suggest.

8. See letter of March 6, 1889, to Victor Delbos: "The rise of Christ is contingent upon, and proceeds in step with, the growth of humanity. And the task of philosophy and apologetics (which, to me, spell one and the same thing) is always this—to

show that He is the greater and escapes all comparisons." And when in 1943 Fr. Teilhard was to use the rather risky word "Super-Christ," this is what he meant too: "By Super-Christ I most certainly do not mean *another* Christ, a second Christ differing from the first and greater than the first. I mean *the same* Christ, the Christ we have known, but who now reveals Himself to us in a form, in dimensions, along contact surfaces, and with an urgency, which are both increased in scope and renewed"; "Super-humanité, Super-Christ, super-charité" (*Œuvres,* t. 9, p. 208). See *infra,* p. 100, note 5; and *Teilhard de Chardin, the Man and His Meaning,* pp. 29–38.

9. During these years, various echoes of what he was reading appear in his letters to Auguste Valensin and J. Wehrlé. His reflections on the mystics culminated in two texts which he wrote in 1925: a long letter to the French Philosophical Society, dealing with Jean Baruzi's thesis on St. John of the Cross (*Bulletin de la Société,* 1925, pp. 85–88); a study of "le problème de la mystique," referred to in note 16.

10. Writing to Mgr. Bruno de Solages, February 16, 1947, and trusting to recollection, Blondel again criticized the Teilhardian method which "reduces itself to a scientific, phenomcnonistic, naturistic frame of reference (as if this frame of reference contained the essential truth) as it treats of material which is also and in fact which is primarily of a metaphysical, religious, and even properly of a supernatural character" (in the Preface we read a later and more favorable judgment). Replying on January 3, Mgr. de Solages pointed out that Fr. Teilhard's system of thought "has progressed a great deal since that time and has overcome earlier shortcomings through 'the within' . . . He writes a fine synthesis of his views on the universe." However, Teilhard's writings do not contain anything equivalent to the chapter in *L'Action* which Blondel devotes to the criticism of scientific activity. Still, one does find observations on the "analytical approach" of science, its success, what it takes for granted, where it falls short. See in particular "Science et Christ, ou analyse et synthèse; Remarques sur la manière dont l'étude scientifique de la matière peut et doit servir à re-

monter jusqu'au Centre divin" (address delivered in Paris, February 27, 1921; *Science et Christ,* pp. 45–62). "Esquisse d'un univers personnel" (1936; *L'Energie humaine,* pp. 72–74).

11. See M. Blondel, *Le point de départ de la recherche philosophique,* second article, "Annales de philosophie chrétienne," t. 152 (June, 1906), pp. 225–249; pp. 230–231: "Therefore one must not judge things as though the apparent fullness of everyday sense perceptions were adequate reflections of the sensible and the real—as would be the case, for example, if one were to find X-rays disconcerting and almost unthinkable in that they would have to be located in a *milieu* which already seems to be full, etc." pp. 244–245: One should avoid "dealing in conceptions derived from sensibility, from positive science, or from metaphysical ideology, their aspirations to ontological truth having been discredited, shown up as mere aspects but not atoms or constituent elements of reality, etc." This idea is treated again later in *La pensée,* t. 1 (1934), in excursus 9 in particular: "Critical remarks on empirical findings as employed in extrapolations leading to subsequent conceptual pictures"; and excursus 10: "Critical remarks on scientific data as they undergo realistic interpretation and lend themselves to metaphysical speculation" (pp. 281–293), etc. Again in *L'Action,* t. 2 (1937), pp. 432–452, excursus 7: "Formal limitations on the scope of science"; and excursuses 8, 9, and 10. Blondel had already treated this problem in Part One of his "Lettre sur les exigences de la pensée contemporaine en matière d'apologétique" in 1896 ("Annales de philosophie chrétienne"): ". . . Just as there is no resemblance between, on the one hand, the qualities of this intuitive data as perceived by the senses and, on the other, the calculations a scientist may make with respect to them, there is no continuity between the scientific symbols and the conceptions of the philosopher . . ." (*Premiers écrits,* 1956, p. 10). He said nonetheless that (p. 11) "It would be incorrect, however, to hold that science does not have a fundamental relationship to these vital questions or that it does not have a role in solving the great problems of our destiny. If it were the place for it here, we would try to work out an en-

tirely new philosophy of science, one which would establish that the theories of positive science, while having no value as material elements in metaphysical constructions, nevertheless are not in essence arbitrary, nor are they detached from the rest of human life which, taken as a whole, constitutes a single problem to be solved."

12. Teilhard does not feel the sharp contrasts in "supernatural" and "physical" as does Blondel; this is because they are out on different tangents and their respective interpretations of "physical" differ thereby. See "Comment se pose aujourd'hui la question du transformisme," in *Etudes,* June 20, 1921: "Christ is the goal, supernaturally, but his role, physically, is the consummation of humanity" (*La vision du passé*). "The new earth (let us say, the Body of Christ) will form a single, physical whole" (letter to Fr. Victor Fontoynont, July 26, 1917; *Pensée religieuse,* p. 353). Teilhard was upset about a theology which, in his opinion, erred in diluting the scriptural and patristic realism with "moralistic" and "legalistic" explanations which "fairly smack of nominalism." (At that time the situation in theology was quite different from what it is now.) He had written (before World War I, in all likelihood) a "Note sur l'union physique entre l'humanité du Christ et les fidèles au cours de la sanctification" (still unpublished; the end seems to have been lost). In 1916 he had written in *La vie cosmique:* "The Mystical Body of Christ should be thought of as a physical reality *without attenuation*"; and "The communion of the saints is fulfilled in blissful union in a physically structured whole" (*Ecrits,* p. 39 and 44).

Several days after this exchange of papers, in a "Note sur le Christ universel" (January, 1920; *Science et Christ*), he was to deplore "the excessive, indiscriminate use of logical, moral, and legalistic relationships in philosophy." "I suppose that the reason why theologians have been blind for so long to the fundamental mystery of the Universal Christ is that their thinking has not been sufficiently dominated by the principle of the *primacy of the organic over the legal*" (pp. 43–44); and p. 39: "By the Universal Christ, I mean Christ the organic center of the entire universe; in other words, the organic center to which all development, even natural, is finally physically suspended, etc." "Esquisse d'un univers personnel" (1936): "From man onward, the construction of the universe proceeds physically through steps of moral greatness"; "It is a love which physically constructs the universe" (*L'Energie humaine,* p. 90). In August, 1943, he was to write in "Super-humanité, super-Christ, super-charité": "Up to the present and despite many statements by St. Paul and the Greek Fathers, theologians have thought of the universal power of Christ in extrinsic and legal terms, etc." (*Science et Christ,* p. 210). See "L'Evolution de la responsabilité dans le monde" (1951; *L'Activation de l'energie,* 221).

This use of the word *physical* is fully justified by the Pauline doctrine which Teilhard often referred to. Fr. Pierre Benoit explains St. Paul's view of "the physical realism of our union with Christ." He analyzes "the very Pauline conception of physical incorporation" into Christ, "a union which is not merely moral but ontological," and goes on to state; "For St. Paul the believer is as fully bound up in the new Adam as is the sinner in the first Adam"; "And why deny our union with Christ and the theme 'the Body of Christ' a physical realism which runs no risk whatever of ending up as gnosis?" (*Exégèse et théologie* [Paris, 1961], pp. 110–116, 125, 158, 164. See *infra,* p. 92, note 35.

Thus Blondel, who saw "more generosity than accuracy" in what Teilhard wrote on this point (in "Mon Univers," 1924), seems to judge his junior too harshly. But he follows up his judgment with ideas which merit serious consideration: "Only a second-rate outlook which will see a polarity in the views of the 'legalists' or notionalists and those of the 'physicists' who are wedded to the concrete and looking *non ad enuntiabilia tantum, sed ad res ipsas, ad finem;* for my part, the *legalists* and *logicalists* express a true and necessary phase grounded in reason and reality; consequently, one is called upon to integrate rather than exclude them, to give one's full attention to the detailed information they offer up, and to pay deference to the intellectual sinew which they furnish the supple life of the universe, a contribution which plays an indispensable role in the accession to morality, personality, and even to religious and mystical truth." We might add that Teilhard's persistent way of seeing a polarity in the legal and the physical (or organic) seems too simple; while he had no liking for "questions of one particular school of thought over another," he may have gotten bogged down in just such a question here, one which is partially outdated and which he doubtless could have avoided, had he been able to stay in closer contact with the philosophical and theological thought of his day.

For Blondel, now as always, the term *physical* designates every reality of this world which comes to hand "*ut sic,*" that is, not yet spiritual transfigured by the coming of the human order, less still by the "*denuo nasci.*" Teilhard goes the same distance; not only does hominisation introduce a sharp change but "nothing of what we are" may remain "*ut sic*": he too will have nothing to do with a "Christian humanism" which would amount to little more than a "naturalism" or, as he says, an "Emersonianism" (see *infra,* p. 111, note 9). Thus the difference between them, while undeniable, is not a matter of the mutual inadmissibility of the other's logic; it lies in the viewpoint customary to each and their respective methods of analysis.

13. This is possibly an allusion to certain passages in "Le milieu mystique" where Teilhard employs the term *seer* (*Ecrits,* p. 140 ss.; 7 times). The word crops up elsewhere too; such as in the "Note sur l'elément universel." It occurs again, in quotation marks, in "Le Christique" (1955, p. 11). See "Comment je vois" (1948), no. 35: ". . . This *cosmic* sense sporadically intense with certain poets and seers. . . ." From a letter of December 13, 1918: "To set oneself up as misunderstood seems ridiculous and conceited. And yet, in truth, (without, I think, the least touch of conceit) I do believe that I can see something, and I would like that something to be seen" (*The Making of a Mind,* pp. 268–269). The influence of St. John of the Cross on Blondel is apparent here.

14. See p. 78, note 10.

15. See Jn. 10, 10: "*Ego veni ut vitam habeant et abundantius habeant.*"

16. See M. Blondel, "Le problème de la mystique," in *Qu'est-ce que la mystique? Cahiers de la Nouvelle Journée,* 3 (1925), pp. 47–51: "How the normally inevitable and inherently incurable failures of human goals in science and in life, hollow out an experimental and philosophical area for the mystic." This study owes much to the work of St. John of the Cross; Blondel had been very interested in him for several years. See also *L'Action* (1893), pp. 347–348, 351–352, and 384: "No one sees God without dying. Nothing touches God without being resuscitated; for no will is good which has not departed out of itself, leaving all the room for the total invasion of His will." Compare with Teilhard: *infra,* p. 85, n. 24 and p. 86, n. 28.

17. Rev. 3, 14; Col. 1, 17; "*Omnia in ipso constant*"; 1, 15: "*primogenitus omnis creaturae.*"

18. Teilhard also often used the word *transformation,* as well as the word *transfiguration,* to designate the passage into the supernatural order. It is an essential word in the Teilhardian dialectic. See certain of the texts quoted in *Pensée religieuse,* pp. 178–183, pp. 186–200, and p. 350. From a letter to Victor Fontoynont, March 15, 1916: "Couldn't the *object* of our human passions, in fact *their very substance,* undergo transformation, undergo mutation into the Absolute, the definitive, the divine?" Or see "Mon univers" (1924); *Science et Christ,* p. 100: Christ saves and beatifies us "by a wonderful transformation." See also "Transformations et prolongements en l'homme du mécanisme de l'évolution" (1951): "Once we discover that the passage from one domain to another is governed by a law of transformation and transposition, how easy it is to clear up the confusion surrounding the living and the human; that is, their relationship to one another and their differences" ("*L'Activation de l'energie*" p. 323). "Le Christique" (1955): the presence of Christ in the universe is a "transforming" presence.

19. Teilhard would have said "reversion" or "excentration"

instead of "a doing away with"; see *infra*, p. 75, note 5; p. 100, note 6; and *The Divine Milieu*, p. 61: "We have not yet crossed the critical point of our excentration, of our reversion to God. There is a further step to take: the one that makes us *lose all foothold within ourselves—oportet illum crescere, me autem minui*. We are still not lost to ourselves. What will be the agent of that definitive transformation? Nothing else than death." See letters of December 8 and 18, 1940, in C. Cuénot, *Teilhard de Chardin* (Baltimore and London, 1965). "Le coeur de la matière" (1950): "Personalized in one fell swoop, simultaneously in its developments which *center us for Christ* and in its diminishments which *ex-centrate us over to Him,* cosmogenesis . . . etc."

20. See Rev. 21, 1.

3.

Pierre Teilhard de Chardin
to Auguste Valensin

1. *Pax Christi* (The Peace of Christ). The customary form of epistolary greeting among members of the Society of Jesus.

2. "The Spiritual Power of Matter," text written at Jersey during during the summer of 1919. In reference to 2 Kgs. 11, 11: "*Cumque incederent simul, ecce currus igneus et equi ignei diviserunt utrumque, —et ascendit Elias per turbinem in caelum*" (And as they went on walking and talking together, behold a fiery chariot and fiery horses parted them both asunder; and of a sudden Elias was caught up by a whirlwind into heaven). Several times a Hymn to Matter was extracted to be published apart (and sometimes incompletely), and consequently exposed to erroneous interpretations. The complete text is found in *Hymn of the Universe* (p. 59). See *infra,* p. 116, note 21.

3. "La vie cosmique" (1916; *Ecrits,* p. 5).

4. See also "Le milieu mystique" (August 13, 1917), "The Circle of His Presence": "Therefore if anyone wants to erect in himself the edifice of a sublime love for God, . . . he must carefully cultivate in himself, by cautious but assiduous intercourse with the deepest realities, the feeling, vision and taste of the Omnipresence which bathes everything in nature in its radiant light. This is the form, the one palpable material, Lord, in which you appear to us, enrapture us, and little by little reveal the marvels of your existence among us" (*Ecrits,* p.

141). Here he is still dealing with the first phase or "circle," however, and not with the third phase which is treated in "La vie cosmique." See "Forma Christi" (1918): "One must truly love the world to feel the desire to transcend it" (*Ecrits*, p. 347).

5. "Critical point"; essential idea; see *supra*, p. 68, note 18, and *infra*, p. 74, note 3. "Le phénomène humain" (1930): "The development of life was regular until it reached a critical point with Man" (*La vision du passé*, p. 233). "L'Esprit de la terre" (1931): "Man . . . establishes himself on earth through a critical point or surface of transformation" (*L'Energie humaine*, p. 34). "La place de l'homme dans la nature" (1932): "Critical or 'singular' points occur everywhere in the movements of matter" (*La vision du passé*, p. 253). "Esquisse d'un univers personnel" (1936): "No psychic magnitude, to our knowledge, can grow indefinitely; at a given moment, it encounters one of these critical points where it changes its state" (*L'Energie humaine*, p. 73). "Trois choses que je vois" (1948): "point of maturation"; "a certain critical state of metamorphosis . . . beyond which we can distinguish nothing of the future, —precisely because it concerns a true 'critical point' of emergence, beyond the temporal-spatial matter of the universe." "La convergence de l'univers" (1951): ". . . some critical and final point of ultra-hominisation" (*L'Activation de l'énergie*, p. 302); "critical thresholds" (p. 297). "La réflexion de de l'energie" (1952): "Taken at its origin, the reflection in each human element . . . corresponds to a critical point separating two kinds of life" (*L'Activation de l'énergie*, p. 352; see pp. 350–351: "superior critical point of planetary reflection"). *The Phenomenon of Man*, p. 78: ". . . critical points have been reached, rungs on the ladder, involving a change of state—jumps of all sorts *in the course of* development"; p. 86: "the need or requirement of a critical point"; p. 102: "a singular critical point of germination"; p. 90: "human critical point"; p. 288: "The end of the world: critical point"; again on pp. 148, 153, 170. Teilhard employs a number of expressions which are all more or less synonymous: "ab-

solute stages" (p. 34), "critical thresholds" (p. 71), "moulting" (p. 80), "evolutionary break" (p. 86), "essential changeover" (p. 89), "critical change" (p. 89), "critical passage" (p. 90), "critical threshold" (p. 170), etc. The result may be the "entirely new" (p. 34), "the beginning of a new order" (p. 79), "a change in the nature (of the state of consciousness)" (p. 89), "a mutation from zero to everything" (p. 171). *The Human Zoological Group* also mentions a "critical point," a "major threshold," and a "point of maturation." "Les singularités de l'espèce humaine" (1955), p. 48. See *The Future of Man* (p. 56): "point of annihilation." See *Pensée religieuse,* p. 185.

6. See "Le milieu mystique": "Lord, that the Spirit may always shine within me, that I may not succumb to the temptation which lies watchful and waiting for all acts of unseemly self-assertion, that I may never forget that you alone are to be sought in everything, —You will send me privations, disappointments, and suffering in the hours that you know best. The object of my love will dwindle, and I will step out beyond it . . ." (*Ecrits,* p. 146). He translated the liturgical formula "*terrena despicere,*" explaining it as "terrenum in terrenis despicere"; he also said: "Disdain for all success or worldly formalities *qua talis,* —but profound esteem for the spiritual substance and organism which is evolving through all of terrestrial life, *in Christo Jesu*" (April 5, 1919).

4.

Teilhard de Chardin's First Paper to Auguste Valensin

1. See note of 1917: "Christ is loved as a person, and imposes Himself as a world." "Le milieu mystique": "The task of grasping the world where it baffles others is reserved for the mystic, the forging of a synthesis where experience and common philosophy fall short and crumble." *Ibid.,* Conclusion: "I think that no one can understand the great mystics, St. Francis, the Blessed Angela, or the others, unless he has truly understood that *Jesus should be loved as a world"* (*Ecrits,* pp. 148 and 169). We note that this is one of the two points where Teilhard "agrees completely" with Blondel. See *Teilhard de Chardin, the Man and His Meaning,* pp. 150–168, for an idea of the complexity and "polyvalency" (his word) of Teilhard's notion of "the world," and an initial analysis of it. Fr. Teilhard speaks of "the world" in quite different ways, depending on whether he means this visible and temporal universe in its actual state, the material universe, or the spiritualized universe, the world of "souls." See, for example, "Note sur le Christ universel" (1920): "Worship of the universal Christ will orient Christian thinking towards this important question which is often lightly dismissed, namely, the value of souls *in se,* that is, the value of the world—in short, the *why* of creation." Or "Mon univers" (1924): "Science necessarily limits itself to studying the material arrangements successively realized by the motion of life. In so doing, it sees only the crust of things. The real evolution of the world takes place in souls, and

in the union of souls. Its inner factors are not mechanistic, but psychological and moral" (*Science et Christ,* pp. 42 and 76–77). We know that soul was an important word for Fr. Teilhard. See "L'Hominisation": "the union of souls" (*La vision du passé,* p. 92). "Sauvons l'humanité": "this dangerous phase which menaces the existence of 'souls' " (*Science et Christ,* p. 189), etc. See *Teilhard de Chardin, the Man and His Meaning,* pp. 167–168.

2. This paragraph was quoted incompletely and out of context, as though it were sufficient to itself, and commented upon erroneously by Dom Georges Frénaud, *Pensée philosophique et religieuse du Père Teilhard de Chardin* (Paris, 1963), p. 38. See *Teilhard de Chardin, the Man and His Meaning,* p. 30.

3. See the quotation from *The Divine Milieu, supra,* p. 68, note 19. The concept of a transformation, of a "critical point" (or "critical threshold": "La convergence de l'univers," 1951; *L'Activation de l'énergie,* p. 297) and death are closely associated. See "La lutte contre la multitude" (1917): "Those will be saved who boldly transpose the center of their being outside themselves, daring to love another more than themselves, becoming this Other in a sense; in other words, journeying through death in search of life. *Si quis vult animam suam salvam facere, perdet eam*" (*Ecrits,* p. 130). Letter of December 28, 1916: "The more I think of it, the more I see that death, through the great invasion and intrusion of everything new that it represents in our individual development, brings freedom and solace, —even in spite of its essentially painful element (because essentially transforming and uprooting). It would be so stifling to feel oneself ineluctably confined to this superficial and experimental facet of our cosmos" (*The Making of a Mind,* p. 158). "Mon univers" (1924): "Sometimes Christ uses our miseries and misfortunes to guide us onto higher paths, where we have the chance to improve ourselves *experimentally.* How many saints became saints through having been defeated in a worldly sphere? But often too, our diminishments and failures do not seem to be offset by any appreciable advantages, even of a spiritual order. At such times, let us trust God more than

ever. The world cannot reach God, *in Christo Jesu,* unless it undergoes a total recasting in which it must appear completely undone, *with no experimental compensation* [of a worldly order] . . ." (*Science et Christ,* pp. 101–102). See *infra* note 5. Retreat of 1940, seventh day (Peking, October 25): "To be in communion with the Becoming *under* the two [inseparable] species: life-death; possession-emergence." Retreat of 1948, first day (Les Moulins, August 30): "The communion through death (the Death Communion)."

4. See "The Great Option" (1939): "mystic annihilation" (in *The Future of Man*). "Forma Christi" (*Ecrits,* p. 349). He later demonstrates that this "excentration" results in a "Super-personalization." See *infra,* p. 89, note 32.

5. See "The Mass of the World" (1923): "If your kingdom, my God, were of this world, I could possess you simply by surrendering myself to the forces which cause us, through suffering and dying, to grow visibly in stature—us or that which is dearer to us than ourselves. But because the term towards which the earth is moving lies not merely beyond each individual thing but beyond the totality of things; because the world travails, not to bring forth from within itself some supreme reality, but to find its consummation through a union with a pre-existing Being; it follows that man can never reach the blazing center of the universe simply by living more and more for himself nor even by spending his life in the service of some earthly cause however great. The world can never be definitively united with you, Lord, save by a sort of reversal, a turning about, an *excentration,* which must involve the temporary collapse not merely of all individual achievements but even of everything that looks like an advancement for humanity. If my being is ever to be decisively attached to yours, there must first die in me not merely the monad ego but also the world: in other words I must first pass through an agonizing phase of diminution for which no tangible compensation will be given me" (*Hymn of the Universe,* New York and London, 1965, pp. 30–31).

6. Note the word *how.* He does not question renunciation itself, or any aspect of it. See "Forma Christi" (1918), Intro-

duction: he could be blundering, and sometimes more than blundering, but he does not wish "to disparage the fundamental tenet of the gratuitous supernatural, or the vital precept of renunciation" (*Ecrits,* p. 336); for "the taste for renunciation": *ibid.,* p. 346. "For the believer, committing oneself to the Absolute entails the obligation of a very strict self-mortification (the suppression of all idle enjoyment and all repose in any sort of pleasure)" (March 18, 1919). Some time later, considering his own spiritual path, he anticipated this objection: "Finally, does it not lead to the same results: devotion, serenity, renunciation, and mysticism . . . as the *via prima?*" (retreat of 1944, fourth day; Peking, October 24). See *infra,* p. 84, note 19.

7. There is some doubt as to whether Fr. Teilhard completely understood St. John of the Cross. See Henri Bouillard, S.J., "La 'sagesse mystique' selon saint Jean de la Croix," in *Recherches de science religieuse,* t. 50 1962), p. 503: "The Spanish friar showed a deep affection for those around him and those responsible to him. He was on guard against feelings tainted with anything of a sensual nature, but added: 'When one's own affections are purely spiritual, their increase spells an increase in God's also.' . . . Then too, he stressed detachment rather than privation in regard to objects and property . . ." However, when one compares the rest of Fr. Bouillard's article with Fr. Teilhard's letter taken as a whole, the differing points of emphasis in the two doctrines become fairly clear. They stem from the fact that St. John was writing for the ordained, whereas Teilhard is trying to offer principles applicable to every situation which a Christian may encounter. But that is not all. Father Teilhard is aware of introducing a new element into the problem, one hitherto unknown to spiritual thinkers, namely, mankind's becoming aware of evolution and the implications, as he saw it, of this new awareness. See *Pensée religieuse,* Ch. 9: "La part de nouveauté." Teilhard is nevertheless critical of "the extreme confusion which merges or identifies the Ineffable of the Vedanta with the Ineffable of St. John of the Cross; it not only delivers up a host of good and defenseless souls to the mirages of the East, but worse, it retards the sorely needed

individualization and birth of a dignified, powerful modern mysticism" ("Comment je vois" [1948], no. 33). At an earlier date, December 17, 1919, he wrote: "Renunciation—it must be shown that the 'annihilation' of St. John of the Cross *is linked* with other levels [states] of Christian life, —as an [the] extreme case, but through the same logic of the completion of the cosmos in God ..."

8. If one were to abstract the concept of "God," the attitude described here would amount to Buddhism, a religion Fr. Teilhard criticized in similar terms in a letter to Fr. de Lubac, October 8, 1933: "I am a strong believer in the rhythm of attachment-detachment. But I feel that the particular, *specific* nature of the Buddhist detachment determines the weaknesses and dangers of the oriental religions. The Buddhist *denies himself* in order to kill desire (he doesn't believe in the value of *being.*) The authentic Christian does the same *by a superabundance* of desire, *a superabundance* of faith in the value of being. It is one of those cases where like appearances conceal conflicting realities." [This same remark was made earlier by Origen, *Contra Celsus,* l. 7, c. 63, regarding certain similarities between the Christian cult and various pagan religions.] See "Le christianisme dans le monde" (1933): "If nothing 'of the breadth, the length, or the height' of the world escapes Christ, the Christian's effort, unlike the Buddhist's, is not to escape things *by avoiding them;* he must *transcend* them by thoroughly exploring, measuring, and conquering them. So that he might enjoy them for himself? Not at all. So that he might extract all the essence of beauty and spirituality that they contain, and return these qualities to God? Exactly." (*Science et Christ,* p. 140. For this "use of creatures," see *The Divine Milieu,* p. 75, note, etc. See p. 85, note 23.) He readily admitted that Buddhism in particular, but also other religions of India, might actually be "less negative" than he had implied, and that "negativism" is probably not inherent to it in its "pure state" (letter to Fr. de Lubac, April, 1934).

9. This scientific term may indicate the source of the vo-

cabulary which Teilhard is to use later on, and sometimes, it seems to us, somewhat indiscriminately.

10. This text is indispensable to our effort to grasp the spiritual problem treated by Fr. Teilhard. See p. 75, note 6. For the various meanings that Teilhard ascribes to the word *world* see *Teilhard de Chardin, The Man and His Meaning,* Part Two.

11. See "Mon univers" (1918): "In order to simplify, let us call: O – the natural conclusion (X) of human and cosmic progress, ω – the supernatural conclusion (the fullness of Christ) of the reign of God.

I conceive of three principal relationships between O and ω:

1. that O and ω are two disparate conclusions [. . .];

2. or that O and ω are two antagonistic conclusions [. . .];

3. or finally, that O and ω are two hierarchal conclusions [. . .]

The first of these three hypotheses seems to me dualistic and ill-conceived [. . .]. The second appeals to me in theory, but in practice it seems to me inhumane and impossible to reconcile: a. with the position of the Church, which has always openly favored and blessed human effort; b. with the most elementary religious psychology, which indicates a close connection between the natural fruition of human faculties and their capacity for love of God [. . .]. I favor then, until advised to the contrary, the third solution . . ." (*Ecrits,* pp. 274–275).

12. This idea will be elaborated in Part One of *The Divine Milieu:* "The Divinization of Our Activities": "Human effort is thus assigned a place in the foreground; the first place, one could say, on the road to perfection" (see also Dom G. Frénaud, *op. cit.,* p. 33). There is an ambiguity here surrounding the expression "the first place" or "the foreground." This letter, and *The Divine Milieu* when read through completely, give one a clear impression that for Teilhard, human effort, while logically and chronologically first, nevertheless does not constitute the essential element of the Christian's spiritual advance. "He sees," says Dom Frénaud (p. 34), "the active period as the first step towards a complete spirituality": this

is more correct, but something still seems to be amiss. A confused understanding comes to light a little further on when the author asks (p. 34): "How are we to take this 'spirituality' of the human effort?", since we have just seen that this effort (even when supernaturalized) only constitutes a first stage of spirituality.

13. See "Le prêtre" (May 26, 1918), Section Three: ". . . You desire my whole being, Jesus, the fruit with the tree, —the work produced and the power harnessed, the *opus* with the *operatio*. To appease your hunger and thirst, to nourish your body to its full development, you must find among us a substance that is fit for you to consume" (*Ecrits,* p. 296). "Note sur le Christ-universel" (January, 1920): "If Christ is universal. . . , human action can be referred to Christ and collaborate in the accomplishment of Christ. All progress, whether in organic life, in scientific knowledge, in the esthetic faculties, or in social consciousness, is therefore Christianizable up to and including the materials in which this progress is realized (because all progress, *in se,* merges organically into the spirit suspended to Christ). This very simple view negates an unyielding and fatal devision in our present-day theories, the separation of the Christian and the human efforts. As human effort becomes divinizable *in opere* (and not just *in operatione*), the world, for the Christian, becomes entirely divine" (*Science et Christ,* pp. 41–42.)

Some people have inferred that for Fr. Teilhard the motive behind an act does not count; that all objectively useful action is "in and of itself" a valuable contribution to the edification of the Body of Christ. This inference has led to the accusation that Teilhard imposes a "fundamentally naturalistic vision" on Christianity. (See *Pensée religieuse,* Appendix 5: "Le P. Teilhard et la morale de l'intention," pp. 364–370.) This is the view of Dom Frénaud (*op. cit.,* p. 33): "The natural effort alone, whatever the motive, as long as this effort is well accomplished and achieved, brings man to God, that is, to Christ." This is a complete misinterpretation. No text of Fr. Teilhard justifies it. There are three points of confusion here: (1) Objectively, even the merely material progress of the world is a good thing; there is, then, an *opus* which is valuable in itself, but this does not mean that if it is carried out without good motives, its author will enjoy a spiritual fruit bringing him closer to Christ. (2) This objective *opus,* of itself, contributes to forming only one of the natural conditions of the completion of the world in Christ. (3) He who acts is in no way excused from having good intentions by his labor (*operatio*), the working materials of his activity (*opus*); in fact it is quite to the contrary. Fr. Teilhard states all of this over and over again. Anyone who reads him closely cannot possibly mistake his thinking on this point. See, for example, "Le prêtre": "If you judge me worthy, Lord, I will show unlimited horizons of humble and unacclaimed effort to those whose lives are banal and drab, and thus their activity, provided the motive is pure, may add a further element to the perfection of the incarnate Word; an element which will be felt by Christ and associated with His immortality" (*Ecrits,* p. 299). Or "Forma Christi" (December, 1918): "*Through our moral intention,* which incorporates us as active members in Jesus Christ, each of our efforts in its totality goes much further than we can ourselves . . ." (*Ecrits,* p. 344). "L'Elément universel" (*ibid.,* p. 411). Or *The Divine Milieu,* p. 119: "Nor is there any limit with respect to the intention which animates our endeavor to act or to accept, because we can always go further in the inward perfecting of our conformity. There can always be greater detachment and greater love." On the other hand, it is clear that there is a certain "natural progress" which "is allied with evil (though it may be recrudescent)": letter to Father Auguste Valensin, July 4, 1920. This view is not specifically Teilhardian. See *infra,* p. 103, note 2.

14. See *The Divine Milieu,* p. 32: "Any increase that I can confer upon myself or upon things is translated into some increase in my power to love and in some progress in Christ's blessed hold upon the universe." To which Dom Frénaud replies (*op. cit.,* p. 35): "No, for supernatural charity is a virtue breathed into us rather than acquired. An increase in our ability

to love Christ can only come about as a gift of grace." This "no" is the result of a misinterpretation. There is most certainly a natural "ability to love," greater or lesser according to the natural development of the human being. Fr. Teilhard clearly distinguishes it from love itself and from supernatural charity. When St. Thomas Aquinas, for example, says that the spiritual being is naturally "*capax Dei*" (capable of God), he is not confusing the natural and supernatural orders any more than does Fr. Teilhard. When he maintains that supernatural charity should not be deprived of "human sap," Teilhard does not reduce charity to this sap; on the contrary, he draws a distinction between them in so doing. Besides, here he is speaking specifically of "supernaturalizable human powers"; see the letter in its entirety. See *The Divine Milieu*, p. 86, note: "The true Christian supernatural, frequently defined by the Church, neither leaves the creature where he is, on his own plane, nor suppresses him: it 'sur-animates' him. It must surely be obvious that, however transcendent and creative they may be, God's love and ardor could only fall upon the *human* heart, that is to say upon an object prepared (from near or from afar) by means of all the nourishments of the earth." See Hans Urs von Balthasar, *Présence et pensée* (Paris, 1942), which summarizes the words of St. Gregory of Nyssa, *De anima et resurrectione*, on the "positive as well as preparatory role of 'passion' and natural love in spiritual ascension. Without this natural passion, 'how else could we be stimulated to strive for celestial things?' "

15. The first period of "action," if it is identified with the "attachment" phase as Fr. Teilhard suggests, is inseparable from the second period (see *infra*). It in no way concerns, as is mistakenly supposed, a concession to pleasure; it is an appeal to effort, to the perfecting of man, to duty. This is the natural basis of supernatural renunciation; the natural condition of a fully Christian spirituality. The effort of "bold conquest" already calls for an initial "protracted detachment": see "La maîtrise du monde et le règne de Dieu" (September 20, 1916), Introduction (*Ecrits*, p. 67–68). "Mon univers" (1924): ". . . the pain of effort. Nothing is more crucifying than effort,

especially spiritual effort, etc." (*Science et Christ,* p. 98). "Human intelligence" is already "an appeal to renunciation" (*Le sens humain,*" February 12, 1929). See also *The Divine Milieu,* p. 77, note: ". . . Once that first choice has been made, the first distinction is drawn between the brave . . . and the pleasure-seekers. . . , between the elect and the condemned." Also p. 40: "In the very optimistic and very broadening attitude which has been roughly sketched above, a true and deep renunciation lies concealed. Anyone who devotes himself to human duty, according to the Christian formula, though outwardly he may seem to be immersed in the concerns of the earth, is in fact, down to the depths of his being, a man of great detachment." See *supra,* p. 66, note 8. We see here the error of those who misunderstand Teilhard's "love of the world," lending his spirituality an unpleasant aura of hedonism, however diluted, purified, or relegated to a secondary role. He was unqualifiedly opposed to all moralities of pleasure (even innocent pleasure). See, for example, his lecture given at Peking on December 28, 1943, "Réflexions sur le bonheur" published in *Les cahiers Pierre Teilhard de Chardin,* vol. 2 (1960), especially pp. 56–58.

16. In other words, "renunciation" is not "a sort of disinterest": "La vie cosmique" (1916; *Ecrits,* p. 8). It would be an error to suppose that it suffers thereby: see *supra,* p. 75, note 6, *infra,* p. 85, note 23. It originates in a "kind of superior indifference (an impassioned indifference) which is born of attachment, in everything, to that which is above everything." Letter of June 10, 1917: "I'm tending . . . to distinguish more sharply the alternating movement that carries the soul towards (and in turn drives it away from) the divine center, homogeneous and essential, through the particular determined forms of the real that we have to know and love and bring into being" (*The Making of a Mind,* p. 195) (see *Pensée religieuse,* p. 41). Pierre Leroy, *Pierre Teilhard de Chardin tel que je l'ai connu* (Paris, 1958), p. 49: He "believes in and practices the Christian doctrine of detachment," but he also tries "to penetrate the structure of renunciation," and it is in this endeavor that he brings forth "a new formula." Hans Urs

von Balthasar, *Prayer* (New York and London, 1962): ". . . The orientation of the spirit towards God does not mean that man can turn his back on the world, but rather implies a certain form of transcendence of the limitations of the carnal and historical *hic et nunc* . . ."

17. For this dialectic of attachment and detachment, see *The Divine Milieu,* p. 70: "First, develop yourself, Christianity says to the Christian. —'First,' in this sense, clearly indicates a priority in nature as much as, or more than, a priority in time. The true Christian should obviously never be *purely and simply* attached to whatever it may, because the contact he seeks with things is always made *with a view to* transcending them or transfiguring them. So that when we speak here of being attached, we mean something penetrated and dominated by detachment." "Mon univers" (1924): ". . . For the Christian dedicated to the unification of the world in Christ, the work of the moral and mystical inner life comes down to two essential complementary movements: the conquest of the world, and escape from it; these two movements are born naturally one from the other, and represent two conjugate forms of a single intention, that of rejoining God through the world" (*Science et Christ,* p. 95). "La parole attendue" (1950), on the "completely synthetic action reunites, corrects, and mutually exalts the spirit of detachment and the spirit of conquest, the spirit of tradition and the spirit of adventurous research, the spirit of the earth and the spirit of God" (*Cahiers Pierre Teilhard de Chardin,* vol. 4, p. 28). *The Divine Milieu:* ". . . This inseparable alliance of two goals: personal progress and renunciation in God; —but there is also a continual and ultimately final preëminence of the second over the first: this is what sums up, in its full sense, the mystery of the Cross." See *Pensée religieuse,* pp. 134–138. M. Barthélemy-Madaule, *Bergson et Teilhard de Chardin,* p. 472.

18. See *infra,* p. 110, note 7, and p. 112, note 12. See "La vie cosmique": "It is true that Jesus cursed the world . . . but the self-satisfied, cowardly, and pleasure-seeking world, not the laboring and self-perfecting world; the egoistic world of

pleasure, not the world of disinterested effort, which could hardly merit God's hatred; for it furthers the impulse of the Creator, lives and progresses, incontestably, in faith in a future that is immanent within it" (*Ecrits,* p. 45). And September 20, 1917: "The false cosmic religions: (1) The comfort-oriented universe (Thackeray); (2) the pleasure-seeking universe; (3) the closed universe . . . (and all egoistic florescences which do not entail true renunciation)."

19. Later, in "L'Atomisme de l'esprit" (September 13, 1941), Fr. Teilhard expressed this idea in somewhat different terms: there are, he indicated, "two pitfalls to avoid in the mystical domain: extenuation and degeneration. 'Omegalisation' will have us pass between this Scylla and Charybdis. Detachment must be realized by an encounter and sublimation, not by rupture. Spiritualization is not attained by negation or evasion of the Multiple, but by *emergence*. This is the '*via tertia*' opening before us when Spirit is no longer the antipode, but the upper pole of matter on the road to super-centration; not the middle road, timid and non-committal, but the upper and daring road, which combines and rectifies the values and properties of the other two roads" (*L'Activation de l'energie,* p. 63). (For this "*via media,*" see *Prière,* I, ch. XI.)

20. Continuation of the same passage of "L'Atomisme de l'esprit": he is speaking of "defining the line of the immutable axis of sainthood." Also see *infra,* p. 118, note 22.

21. See letter to Fr. Victor Fontoynont, March 15, 1916: "I have been thinking over and jotting down some ideas on a subject which has always been the problem of my inner life—a little like the question of Rome for Newman or the meaning of the callings of the soul for Psichari—I mean the reconciliation of progress and detachment; of ardent and legitimate love for a greater earth on the one hand, and a single-minded pursuit of the kingdom of heaven, on the other. How can we be as Christian as possible and at the same time as human as possible?" (*Pensée religieuse,* p. 349). See *infra,* p. 82–83, note 39.

22. "The one thing necessary" (Lk. 10, 42). Throughout his life Fr. Teilhard made frequent use of this expression; he proba-

bly owes it to Blondel: *L'Action* (1893), pp. 339–356: "L'Unique nécessaire"; see *L'Itinéraire philosophique de Maurice Blondel* (1928), p. 41. Teilhard, letter of August 14, 1918: ". . . As it says in the Gospel for the feast [Assumption], we'll try, both of us, to attach ourselves ever more firmly to the possession and, in a way, the indwelling, of the *'unum necessarium'* " (*The Making of a Mind,* p. 226). "The Spiritual Power of Matter" (*Hymn of the Universe,* p. 68). Letter of August 27, 1931: ". . . I find I can only immerse myself in the One Thing Necessary" (*Letters from a Traveller,* p. 183), etc. The word reappeared several times in the Notes written during his retreats. Sometimes it is simply equivalent to God; at other times the sense is defined and determined by the context and by the whole of the Teilhardian spirituality. It has synonyms: "the One Interest," "the One Sufficiency," "the One Essential" ("Le milieu mystique"), etc. See *Pensée religieuse,* pp. 40–41.

23. Thus, as he said during his retreat of 1940 (first day; Peking, October 19): "True 'indifference' is the passion for participating *solely* with the Omega in beings—a passion for beings as Omegalized and Omegalizable creatures." See *supra,* p. 82, note 16. This idea was inspired by the St. Ignatius of Loyola's *"tantum quantum,"* given in the *Spiritual Exercises* as a rule pertaining to the use of creatures. Teilhard alludes to this "basic problem of the use of creatures" in *The Divine Milieu,* p. 75, note. But there is an additional element here, because he was thinking not only of things but of people who are loved for their being united with God or for being called to the divine union. See letter to Fr. Auguste Valensin, December 31, 1926: "I continue to find no further taste for things outside of their relation to the universal Christ." For Blondel's concept of "indifference" see M. Ossa, *loc. cit.,* pp. 192–201.

24. Hence the privileged importance of death, in Teilhardian thought, as a profound and *total* metamorphosis. See *infra,* p. 95, note 39; p. 100, note 6.

25. Here again we have the traditional distinction between the natural and the supernatural. "Christianizable," "super-

naturalizable," "divinizable" (and "Omegalizable") are Teil-hardian expressions, correlative (and antithetical) to Christian-ized or Christian, supernaturalized or supernatural, divinized or divine (and "Omegalized").

26. See *The Divine Milieu.* In "Le coeur de la matière" (1950) he points out that "the direction of God's will rapidly takes on importance in one's *own* spiritual life." See letter to Claude Rivière, Peking, December 14, 1942 (Claude Rivière, *Teilhard, Claudel et Mauriac,* 1963, pp. 47–48). *The Making of a Mind,* pp. 67, 70, 73, 158. "L'Elément universel" (*Ecrits,* p. 405–406), etc. On March 22, 1916, he told of having experi-enced "a great loving impulse for the Will of God as it en-velops and carries us along, sometimes by the implacable evolu-tion of organic ills, sometimes by disappointments of fate, sometimes by the weaknesses of our nature." His aim was al-ways "to be faithful to what God asks of me" (July 11, 1932). Writing to his superior general, on October 12, 1951, he spoke of his decision to remain an "obedient child" (in Pierre LeRoy, S.J., *Pierre Teilhard de Chardin tel que je l'ai connu,* Paris, 1958, p. 58). To another of his superiors, he wrote (February 16, 1953): "You know that you can tell me anything, and that I will do everything that you tell me." Fidelity, along with purity and faith, is one of the three forces effecting "the individual steps of progress of the divine Milieu." See *Pensée religieuse,* p. 321, note 6.

27. Once again he is specifying that if the *opus* (the work realized) plays an indispensable role in "the completion of Christ," it does so only by preparing for Him "a material more or less close at hand." Therefore this is the sense, and the only sense, in which the *opus* "contributes to the realization of the kingdom of God" or that it constitutes "a contribution to the completion of the Body of Christ"; in other words, its effect is quite indirect (Frénaud, *op. cit.,* pp. 8 and 32). This negates the objections of Dom Frénaud. See *supra,* p. 79, note 13. For "Pleroma" see *infra,* p. 92, note 35.

28. For the concept of "passivities" see *The Divine Milieu,* Part Two. "The immobile action" functions through them, as

well as through inner purity and contemplation. This is where exterior activity itself should lead. See "Note pour servir à l'évangélisation des temps nouveaux" (1919), on the third period of the "complete cycle of inner life": "*sublimate* human effort by making it reach out (through a prolongation of itself) to the higher forms of activity; namely, purity, contemplation, and death *in God*" (*Ecrits,* p. 380). Letter of December 5, on the Immaculate Conception (*The Making of a Mind,* pp. 148–150). "La signification et la valeur constructrice de la souffrance" (1933; *L'Energie humaine,* pp. 64–65). "Quelques réflexions sur la conversion du monde" (1936): "Detachment does not consist in condemnation and rejection, but in an encountering, a dealing with, and a sublimation" (*Science et Christ,* p. 162). "L'Energie spirituelle de la souffrance" (1950; *L'Activation de l'energie,* pp. 255–257), etc. See *Pensée religieuse,* pp. 43–46; *Prière,* pp. 73–79. And Bernard Besret, S.O. Cist., *Incarnation ou eschatologie?* (Paris, 1964), pp. 216–221, which gave a clear picture of Fr. Teilhard's teachings on "passivities" and the spiritual fruitfulness of an apparent defeat; these teachings are often overlooked.

See letter of January 29, 1917: ". . . And is it not as beautifying to feel the influence of Him we love exert itself to make us less (as his wisdom plans) rather than greater? —To go back to Blondel's words that you copied for me, 'the action of others on ourselves' is more clearly seen in sorrow than in enjoyment, and the same is thus true of the resulting joy" (*The Making of a Mind,* p. 176). And earlier, on December 28, 1916 (p. 158), he wrote: " 'The joy of other's action in ourselves,' that's exactly what makes the passivities of existence seem so sweet to me, so worthy of adoration (since it is through them that God asserts his primacy over us)—so much so that if I didn't react against this feeling I'd forget that every creature's success is bound up with its active good will, and that no immanent inevitability drives us towards success." These early texts come to mind as one reads his letter of February 24, 1953, to his friend George B. Barbour, who had just lost his son: "[In the experience you have just had] you will know how to recognize and *adore* a higher form of love" (George B. Barbour, *In the Field with Teilhard de Chardin,* New York, 1965, p. 147). See *infra,* p. 103, notes 1 and 2.

29. See *supra,* p. 79, note 13; p. 86, note 27.

30. Though Fr. Teilhard was trying to define and justify his own "path," he did not, we note, regard it as the only one leading to God. See *Le Prêtre* (1918): "Innumerable are the voices and levels of your call. The vocations you summon us to are essentially diverse. Each region, nation, and social category needs its own apostle . . ." (*Ecrits,* p. 298). On the fourth day of his retreat of October, 1940, meditating on the Epiphany, he wrote: "Stella; Jesus, Maria. Grace: to follow *my* light, my special vocation." See *The Divine Milieu,* p. 75; "What has been said of individuals must be transposed and applied to the Church as a whole. It is probable that the Church is led, at different times in the course of her existence, to emphasize in her general life now a greater care to collaborate in the earthly task, now a more jealous concern to stress the ultimate transcendence of her preoccupations, etc."

31. See *supra,* p. 65, note 4. The word *annihilation* occurs frequently in mystical language. It is found in a Latin prayer Fr. Teilhard was fond of quoting: *"Tu Domine, include me in imis visceribus Cordis tui, atque ibi me detine, excoque, expurga, accende, ignifac, sublima, ad purissimum Cordis tui gustum atque placitum, ad puram annihilationem meam"* (You, my Lord, enclose me in the deepest entrails of your Heart, and hold me there, burn me, purify me, inflame me, transfigure me to the perfect satisfaction of your tastes, to the utter annihilation of myself) (letter of September 23, 1917; *The Making of a Mind,* p. 203). He attributes this prayer to "one of our sixteenth-century Fathers"; we have not been able to identify the source. The word comes up again in *The Divine Milieu,* p. 60: ". . . If, as we are convinced, this annihilation in the other must be more complete the more we attach ourselves to something greater than ourselves, then we cannot set limits to the sacrifice required of us on our journey to God." "Self-effacement" [*anéantissement*] has a similar meaning and is also common in

mystical language. Fr. M. Viller remarked that it was used twenty times by St. Catherine de Gênes (*Revue d'ascétique et de mystique*, 1934, p. 389). Bérulle also used it (see Jean Orcibal, *Le cardinal de Bérulle*, 1965, p. 41; R. Bellemare, *Le sens de la créature dans la doctrine de Bérulle*, 1959, p. 62), as well as Gagliardi, etc.; and Fr. de Foucauld: "Our self-effacement is the most powerful means we have for uniting ourselves with Jesus and for benefiting other souls" (letter to Marie de Bondy, December 1, 1916; in J. Fr. Six, *Itinéraire spirituel de Charles de Foucauld*, 1958, p. 65); also Péguy (*Eve*):

". . . Could You receive in Your eternity . . .

the humiliation of our humanity";

etc. St. John Eudes, like Teilhard, speaks of "self-effacement" in connection with the Heart of Jesus: see Paul Micent, "Le Coeur du Christ selon Teilhard de Chardin et selon saint Jean Eudes," in *Notre vie eudiste*, April, 1965, pp. 204–209.

32. A moment ago, Fr. Teilhard referred to this "supernatural depersonalization" as the "eminent transformation of the personality." His early essays do not bring out this second aspect as they might. It was not until 1930 or thereabouts that Fr. Teilhard made what he himself called "the discovery of the personal" in his systematic thought. From then on, he did all he could to show convincing proof that "evolution, even when seen objectively, has been moving towards the creation of personal centers," and that "just as the laws of the world of spirits, that is, the laws of the personal, seem by a sort of countershock, to be in some way dominating all evolution in advance, so do they appear to have a hyper-personal, not an impersonal, quality about them, stemming from the beyond." But in 1917 he wrote: "Never has my vocation seemed clearer to me than it is now, stripped of its unessentials: it is to personalize the world in God." That same year he began drafting "Le milieu mystique," dividing it into five parts and entitling the last part "The Sphere of the Personal" (*Ecrits*, p. 163).

July 15, 1929: "In my view of the world 'the spiritual' and, following close upon it, 'the personal' are ideas of great importance, ideas growing everywhere in influence and scope." 1931:

"From man onward, everything in the universe enters into personalized being." November 15, 1935: "The universe is an immense thing; we would be lost in it if it did not converge in the personal." 1937: "Christianity, faced with a humanity which may allow everything it has gained to slip over into the 'second matter' of philosophic determinisms and social processes, faced with a humanity which may lose everything of itself which the progress of life has awakened, maintains the primacy of reflective thought, in other words, the primacy of personalized thought." 1941: "Finally, we cannot find the generative principle of our unification by restricting ourselves to the contemplation of a single truth or in restricting ourselves to desire for a single Something; it is to be found in a general attraction emanating from a single Being." 1950: "At no time in my life have I found the least difficulty in addressing God as a supreme *Someone*." Other texts in *Pensée religieuse,* Ch. 13: "Personalism." See *Prière,* pp. 24–30. This word *personalism* was Teilhard's, as in "Sauvons l'humanité, réflexions sur la crise présente" (Peking, November 11, 1936; *Science et Christ,* pp. 178 and 182), etc.

Fr. Teilhard often tried to throw light on this law, whereby "union differentiates," and ends up personalizing the entities at hand. In *The Phenomenon of Man* he showed that "the only universe capable of containing the human person is an irreversibly 'personalizing' universe," etc. (p. 290). See O. Rabut, O.P., *Teilhard de Chardin* (New York and London, 1961). There is a certain convergence between the personalist doctrine elaborated by Teilhard and the doctrine Blondel discusses in his "Les equivoques du personnalisme" (*Politique,* March, 1934). See Maurice Nédoncelle, "Maurice Blondel et 'Les equivoques du personnalisme,' " in *Teoresi,* 1950.

33. This doctrine seems to fall into line with St. Paul's teachings on the "cosmic role" of Christ: see Ferdinand Prat, S.J., *The Theology of St. Paul* 2 vols. (Westminster [Md.] and London, 1946), Joseph Huby, *Saint Paul, Les epîtres de la captivité* (1935), p. 42, etc. See *Prière,* pp. 39–50. In "Mon univers" (1924) Fr. Teilhard speaks of the subterfuge "by which timid

minds think to escape the formidable realism" of St. Paul and St. John, by claiming that "the cosmic attributes of the Pauline Christ belong to the Divinity alone" (*Science et Christ,* pp. 82–83). As Teilhard points out a little further on, this does not contradict the idea that the Incarnation took place "*solely* for our supernaturalization." He explained this point in "L'Union créatrice" (1917), 7: "Certainly, every earthly thing cannot look to Christ as the center, cannot naturally aspire to marry Him. Destination in Christ is an unforeseen and gratuitous favor of the Creator. The truth is this, that the universe has been so thoroughly *recast* in the supernatural by the Incarnation that, speaking in concrete terms, we cannot seek nor imagine any other center which the elements of this world could have gravitated towards, without this elevation to grace . . ." (*Ecrits,* p. 195). In "Mon univers" (1924) he went on to explain: "The Cosmos could never have been conceived and realized, had it not had a supreme Center of spiritual consistency . . . The presence of an Omega at its head has no bearing on the fact of its 'supernatural elevation.' The 'gracious' characteristic of the world stems from the fact that the universal Center was not assigned to some sort of supreme intermediary between God and the universe, but was taken by the Divinity itself, —who introduced us thus, '*in et cum Mundo,*' into the Trinitary bosom of its immanence" (*Science et Christ,* p. 84). See *supra,* p. 61, note 5; *Prière,* pp. 39–50. See letter to Fr. Auguste Valensin, January 10, 1920: "It would be impossible to understand a Christ organically *central* in the supernatural universe, and in physical juxtaposition to the natural universe."

34. "On a forward tilt" is a Teilhardian expression, used both in his theory of cosmic evolution and his doctrine of spirituality. The expression "the world with all its weight bears on a center lying in front of it" is a correlative image ("Allocution de mariage," 1928); ". . . a world in which physical equilibrium is maintained by a laborious pitching forward into ever greater consciousness and personalization" (letter to Fr. Valensin, February 25, 1929). "L'Union créatrice" (1917): "The characteristic of a convergent evolution. . . , is that Being makes

its appearance in a 'forward tilt,' so to speak." Nothing supports the world from behind, since it tends to break away from the crumbling which is necessarily going on there. Things are held by their movement forward" (*Ecrits,* p. 182). See letter of Easter, 1927: ". . . This important act, not only of death but of life, consists in resting off balance, leaning on Him who holds and supports us, etc." "L'Energie d'évolution": ". . . thrown forward on entropy" (*L'Activation de l'énergie,* p. 388). "La mystique de la science" (*Etudes,* March, 1939): "We find ourselves here in the ruins of materialism, pitched forward by the combined impetus of our needs and hopes" (*L'Energie humaine* p. 218). "Esquisse d'un univers personnel": ". . . Everything is tilting forward onto Him (God), and He onto nothing" (*L'Energie humaine* p. 88). An expression with the same meaning in "La convergence de l'univers": "A world held in equilibrium by the unstable" (*L'Activation de l'énergie* p. 33). *Man's Place in Nature,* p. 24*: ". . . The whole of biology is thrown forward onto itself, wth no intelligible connection with the rest of physics"; p. 31: "corpuscles . . . each overlapping its predecessor—progressing towards a fulfillment still to be attained." He also wrote of himself, in a difficult moment: "It isn't easy to live like this, thrown forward onto the future" (letter to Fr. de Lubac, Paris, September 18, 1948).

35. A Pauline term, adopted by Teilhard. (See "L'Elément universel," *Ecrits,* pp. 408 and 412. *The Divine Milieu,* pp. 125 and 143. "La parole attendue" [1940], in *Cahiers Pierre Teilhard de Chardin,* vol. 4, p. 26). See especially Col. 1, 19: "For it pleased the Father that in Him [Christ] should all fullness dwell"; and 2, 9: "For in him dwelleth all the fullness of the Godhead bodily, and ye are complete in him, which is the head of all principality and power . . ." It is difficult to pin down the meaning of this word. See Pierre Benoit, O.P., article on "Paul" (Epistle of St.) in the *Supplément au Dictionnaire de la Bible* (compiled and edited by H. Cazelles and A. Feuillet), t. 7, col. 164: "In this context we may justifiably imagine a 'Pleroma' of the whole universe, not just one limited to the divine essence alone; that is, both the divinity and the cosmos

as it has been gathered in by means of the Body of Christ. Through the Incarnation and the Resurrection, Christ is both God and Man, and His fullness harbors a saving God and those who are saved, yet goes still further to include those select ranks of humanity, including the angelic powers, which serve to make up the cosmos." And col. 203: In the Epistle to the Ephesians, "where the importance of this section of humanity has declined and where the Church is on the rise, a force pervading everything, the term *pleroma* has lost its former attributes. Now, accordingly and by degrees, it comes to be associated with the Church itself. This Church is not just the Body of Christ, but His Pleroma too. Strictly speaking, her members constitute the Body, but the Church goes beyond that somehow to incorporate within herself all the forces of a regenerated creation (see Rom. 8, 21), a creation suffused with the energies of the resuscitated Christ who completely fills the universe (4, 10) and is filled by it in turn (1, 23)." See Eph. 1, 23: "[The Church] which is His Body, the fullness of him that filleth all in all." Fr. Benoit refers to an article entitled "Pleroma" to be published in the near future. Also see "Corps, Tête et Plerôme," in *Exégèse et Théologie* (1961), t. 2, especially pp. 135–153. Theodore of Mopsuestia has discussed the cosmic nature of the Pauline Pleroma; "the great virtue" of his interpretation "lies in its establishing the meaning of the word as it was used in St. Paul's day, the meaning current in literary trends he was familiar with," namely, in literature derived from Stoic philosophy, and in the Septuagint version of the Bible (see pp. 142–144). See also J. Dupont, *Gnosis* (Paris, 1949), pp. 453–476. M. Bogdasavich, O.S.B., "The Idea of Pleroma in the Epistles to the Colossians and Ephesians," in *The Downside Review,* April, 1965, pp. 118–130.

Blondel too wanted to retain the word *Pleroma,* though he was very cautious in his use of it. See his letter to Fr. Auguste Valensin, March 26, 1935: ". . . I would like to lead my readers to a concept of a real order which prepares the lower forms of existence for an integration, a final merging into what the Bible calls *caelum novum, novam terram,* and *resurrectionem carnis.*

I feel there is something illuminating and useful in this word *pleroma,* in the meaning it had back in the early days of Christian thought. Don't you think it would be an apt term if it were shorn of its Gnostic associations, for designating the full execution of the plan of creation and redemption?" (Blondel-Valensin, *Correspondance,* t. 3, 1965, pp. 196–197).

See C. F. Mooney, "The Body of Christ in the Writings of Teilhard de Chardin," *loc. cit.,* p. 604: "For many exegetes today the 'Plenitude' of Christ in this extraordinary text [Col. 1, 15–20], His Pleroma, represents in Paul's mind the extension of Christ's work of redemption to the whole cosmos, the whole of creation. The term itself was quite common in the Stoic vocabulary of the time, and designated God's penetration and envelopment of the material world. In Colossians and Ephesians, Paul strips it of its Stoic pantheism and gives it a content familiar to the Old Testament, that of the cosmos filled with the creative presence of God. The 'fulness' which resides in Christ, therefore, is 'the plenitude of being,' including both the fulness of divinity and the fulness of the universe. Christ is God, and through His work of redemption He unites to Himself not only redeemed humanity, for which Paul reserves the term *Body,* but also the whole of the cosmos which is humanity's dwelling place."

In his "Note sur l'union physique entre l'humanité du Christ et les fidèles au cours de la sanctification," Teilhard spoke of "the consummation of the Mystical Body (that is, the Pleroma of St. Paul)." See letter of September 21, 1929, from Peking: "A vast *Opus* is maturing in the world, which, purified by 'death,' is destined for *integration* into the Pleroma."

36. See "L'Elément universel" (1939): "If I had to choose a single word which would characterize 'spirit' and the plan of action of one who has seen the Universal Christ smiling at the conclusion of all things, I would adopt the term *integrism,* an expression which ought normally, if taken in the narrow sense in which it has been employed, to be shunned; but I am speaking of *integrism in purity*—meaning first of all the authentic Christ, Christ in His truth and supernaturalness. This is the

only form in which Jesus has the virtue of conquering and incorporating the world. —But also *integrism in universality!* That there will not be a single element of force, not one iota of the salvable world which may escape integration into the fullness of Jesus! . . . —We must see to it that Jesus reigns there, yes, especially there in those fringe areas of the world which are continually being born, so that no chosen particle may escape the Pleroma (nothing is so small that it plays an accessory role within the totality), but then too, so that the universe may truly be forming *under the influence* of Christ . . . —First and foremost, Christ in His integrity" (*Ecrits,* pp. 412–413). Later, pained by the "integrist movement," he wrote with respect to the above quotation, "I recall a thought I had more than ten years ago. This movement seeks to associate Christian orthodoxy with an 'integrism,' that is, with a respect for the least bits of clockwork of a tiny microcosm conceived centuries ago. —But actually, the true Christian ideal is 'integralism,' that is, an application of the Christian directives to the totality of resources contained in the world" (to Léontine Zanta, May 20, 1924; May 7, 1927). See *supra,* p. 90, note 33, and p. 62, note 7.

37. See *The Phenomenon of Man,* pp. 270–271, on Omega: "While being the last term of its series, it is also outside all series . . . If by very nature it did not escape from the time and space which it gathers together, it would not be Omega . . . Autonomy, actuality, irreversibility, and thus finally transcendence are finally the four attributes of Omega."

38. See "L'Eternel féminin" (1918): ". . . The center of that which drew you to me shifts, moves imperceptibly towards the pole where all the directions of spirit converge. . . . Now it is God who waits for you in me!" (*Ecrits,* p. 260). "Esquisse d'un univers personnel" (1936; *L'Energie humaine,* pp. 93–96).

39. See *The Divine Milieu,* p. 103. ". . . the effort required of our fidelity must be consummated *beyond a total transformation* of ourselves and of everything around us. "La lutte contre la multitude" (1917): "Who can describe the anguish of this metamorphosis?" (*Ecrits,* p. 131). See *infra,* p. 100, note 6; *supra,* p. 84, note 24; *The Divine Milieu,* p. 86, note 1: "It is

astonishing that so few minds should succeed . . . in grasping the notion of transformation. Sometimes the thing transformed seems to them to be the old thing unchanged; at other times they see in it only the entirely new. In the first case, it is the spirit that eludes them; in the second case, it is the matter. Though not so crude as the first excess, the second is shown by experience to be no less destructive of the equilibrium of mankind." In spite of these and many other similar texts, a pamphleteer has seen fit to make this pronouncement: "Father Teilhard failed to perceive the second outcome of the act of incarnation, that is, transformation" (Bernard Charbonneau, *Teilhard de Chardin, prophète d'un age totalitaire* [Paris, 1963], p. 212). The words *transformation* and *metamorphosis* occur often in *The Phenomenon of Man*.

40. *The Divine Milieu* will take this idea as its prime assumption and go on from there. And in some sense this is also true of Teilhard's spirituality and apologetics. See also the "Note pour servir à l'évangelisation des temps nouveaux" (1919), and the "Note sur la notion de perfection chrétienne" (1942). See letter to Fr. Auguste Valensin, Holy Saturday, 1922: ". . . If I could only play some small role in this great cause—the only one which speaks to the depths of my being—that of the explicit fusion of Christian life with the 'natural' sap of the universe." And on December 26, 1926, he wrote to Fr. Valensin about "the fusion of two great loves, God and world." "Sur la valeur religieuse de la Recherche" (Versailles, 1947): "Truly, if there is anyone who can effectively *in actu et in vivo* synthesize the two faiths confronting each other in the world today, it will be, by dint of tradition and training, the sons of St. Ignatius—but this can only be achieved (and this is an essential condition) if they have absorbed once and for all this fundamental truth which expresses (if I am not deluding myself) the essence and necessities of the 'modern mind'; namely, that the Reign of Christ we are dedicated to can only be established on an earth carried to the extremes of its humanization *through all the channels of its technology and thought*" (*Science et Christ,* p. 263).

5.

Maurice Blondel to Auguste Valensin

1. *Confessions,* 1. XI, c. 30, n. 40: *"Et stabo atque solidabor in te, in forma mea, veritate tua . . ."* ("Then will I be stable and solid in you, in my true form, your Truth").

2. See P. Teilhard, "Mon univers" (1918): "For me, the best philosophy will always be the one which will enable me to have a stronger sense of Christ as a necessary force pervading everything" (*Ecrits,* p. 277). And "Mon univers" (1924): "I cannot read St. Paul without finding the universal and cosmic domination of the Incarnate Word shining forth in what he is saying" (*Science et Christ,* p. 84).

3. See *supra,* pp. 66–67, note 7.

4. *Bulletin de la Société française de philosophie,* t. 6, session of October 26, 1905, "Le développement des états mystiques chez sainte Thérèse" (by H. Delacroix); pp. 19–23, letter to M. Blondel, pp. 21–22: "If the personal consciousness of St. Theresa were heightened rather than reduced, if it proceeded through mystical stages or managed to maintain itself in higher states by virtue of growing larger, surer of itself, more dispossessed, more in conformity with the very definition of personality (namely, *consciousness of the impersonal*), more perfectly adapted to complex difficulties, more capable of actions which, while sometimes seeming reckless from a human point of view, nonetheless end in triumph over the trials at hand in the miraculous accomplishment of enduring plans—in short, if this consciousness manifested qualities which have not the slightest resemblance to the mental stigmata of neurosis—

would we have the right to maintain that what Maine de Bilan called the third life satisfies the conditions of the first life?"

5. M. Blondel approached the question from another angle in "Le problème de la mystique," *loc. cit.* (1925), pp. 53–57: "How reason survives and still functions in the highest forms of mystical union." See *supra,* p. 68, note 16.

6. Blondel went quite thoroughly into this notion of an "unnaturalizable supernatural" and coined many terms for putting it across. See p. 101, note 9.

7. L. XI, c. 29, n. 39: "... *Praeterita oblitus, non in ea quae futura et transitura sunt, sed in ea quae ante non distentus, sed extensus, non secundum distentionem, sed secundum intentionem sequor ad palmam supernae vocationis, ubi audiam vocem laudis et contempler delectationem tuam nec venientem nec praetereuntem."* — "... *donec in te confluam purgatus et liquidus igne amoris tui."* "Forgetting the past, turned not towards future and transitory things, but towards those before me, and towards which I am not distended but stretched, I follow my path, in an effort not of distention but of intention, towards the crown calling me from above, that I might hear there the voice of praise, and contemplate your delights which have neither beginning nor end." — "... until the day when I empty into You, purified and liquified in the fire of your love."

Blondel was fond of this text by St. Augustine. He was to draw inspiration from it again, specifically on p. 100 of *L'Etre et les êtres* where he quotes it loosely, just as he did above, and just as St. Augustine himself had quoted St. Paul (Eph. 3, 13–14): "... St. Augustine brought out the dominant feature of this impassioned, fragmented life, this existence distended through everything; left to its natural activities, he says, our spirit is *distentus per omnia dilaceretur."* See Jules Chaix-Ruy, "Maurice Blondel et saint Augustine," in *Revue des études augustiniennes,* 11 (1965), pp. 55–84. Aimé Forest, "L'Augustinisme de Maurice Blondel," in *Sciences ecclésiastiques,* 14 (1962), pp. 175–193.

6.

Maurice Blondel's Second Paper
to Auguste Valensin

1. This is a problem of the critique of knowledge; Blondel spoke to it *supra*, pp. 23–24. Teilhard never made solid contact with it, and may not have fully understood its terms. It held no great interest for him, even though it could have had some bearing on the central question of his thought.

2. This passage echoes the general spirit we encounter in the final pages of the "Lettre sur les exigences de la pensée contemporaine en matière d'apologétique" (1896; *Les premiers écrits de Maurice Blondel* [Paris, 1956], pp. 89–95).

3. Teilhard too was drawn to St. Francis of Assisi and made reference to him in his writings and letters: letter to Fr. Auguste Valensin, December 31, 1926; and again to Fr. Valensin on June 21, 1921; *The Divine Milieu*, p. 104. See letter to Marguerite Teillard, October 4, 1917 (*The Making of a Mind*, pp. 206–208.

4. The mentality briefly described here was one of the principal questions discussed in *La semaine sociale de Bordeaux et le monophorisme*, an extract from the *Annales de philosophie chrétienne* (252 pp., 1910). With these statements Blondel gives us a picture of what Teilhard was reacting against at the time; these reactions led Teilhard to take his stand on the value of human effort. If they are not understandable to many people today, it is certainly because the mentality in the Church is no longer what it was; consequently, Teilhard will seem to go too

far at times, not attuned to the present-day situation. See Claude Tresmontant, *Pierre Teilhard de Chardin* (Baltimore and London, 1956), p. 104: "... Teilhard was merely struggling against a caricature [of Christian spirituality], but this caricature is unfortunately only too real." This was even truer in certain circles half a century ago.

5. On March 13, 1889, Blondel had written, "For [spiritual detachment], we find that the will of God Himself is dwelling in all things, His will alone; but this, in and of itself, warrants man's forming a very pure attachment to all being and to all knowledge. Now the task at hand is to study and to justify the sanctity of life as it is bound up with nature and with a very human knowledge; we should not pursue our devotions with a deaf ear to mankind's needs or to the scientific and metaphysical conquest of the world" (*Carnets intimes,* pp. 183–184). See Etienne Gilson, *Philosophy and Theology* (New York, 1962), pp. 234–235: "We are witnessing today a marvel, a changing of the face of nature. Christian philosophy must take it into account. [. . .] The Church is so certain of the truth of faith, that to her any increase in knowledge represents the promise of an inevitable corresponding increase in the intellection of faith, which is the very substance of Christian philosophy. Let us never forget St. Paul: *Invisibilia Dei* . . . The better we know nature, the better we can know God." This is the principle of the *Deus semper major,* —of Teilhard's "even greater Christ." In a letter of October 10, 1950, he declared himself "wholly committed to the effort of developing a Christology truly worthy of the immense, organic universe impressing itself on the modern human consciousness." Writing to Fr. André Ravier on October 10, 1950, he expressed regret at having observed that many in the Church "are not conscious of what the universe has become within a century: spatially, temporally, and *organically.*" See *supra,* p. 77, note 8.

6. See P. Teilhard, "Le milieu mystique": "A transformation is in the making; this is more than a simple union—human activity can only make ready and humbly accept." (*Ecrits,* pp. 161–162). *The Divine Milieu,* p. 61: "God must, in some way

or other, make room for Himself, hollowing us out and emptying us, if He is finally to penetrate into us . . . The function of death is to provide the necessary entrance into our innermost selves." To Léontine Zanta, August 22, 1928: "What a strange, capricious force, the heart! Nowhere do we feel life as rich, as ebullient and confused. How can we transfigure this force without impoverishing it?" See retreat of 1941: "The exercise of omnipresence on transfiguration."

7. See Rom. 8, 18: *"Existimo enim quod non sunt condignae passiones hujus temporis ad futuram gloriam, quae revelabitur in nobis."* "For I reckon that the sufferings of this present time are not worthy to be compared with the glory which shall be revealed in us."

8. See *infra,* p. 105, note 3, and p. 109, note 6.

9. Here again Blondel is stressing his idea of the unnaturalizable supernatural. See *Vocabulaire technique et critique de la philosophie,* by André Lalande (5th ed., 1947), pp. 1053–1054, note on "Blondel": ". . . In a strict sense the term *supernatural,* a word whose origins and usage stem from the Christian language, refers to a gratuitous condescendence proceeding from God, elevating the intelligent being to a state which cannot be the *natural state* of any created being; a state which could neither be realized nor merited, nor even expressly conceived by any *natural* force: for it involves the communication of the inner divine life, *secretum Regis,* truth impenetrable to all philosophical views, a goodness beyond all aspirations of the will. Initiating us into the mystery of His Trinity, the hidden God reveals to us the divine processions, the generation of the Word by the Father, the spiration of the Holy Spirit by the Father and the Son; and through love He invites all men to participate in His nature and His beatitude, making them *divinae consortes naturae,* etc." See also *Exigences philosophiques du Christianisme* (Paris, 1950), vol. 1, *Le sens chrétien,* Chs. 7 and 10–12. *L'action,* t. 2 (1937), excursus 35, pp. 513–523.

At the same time, Blondel shows up the incompleteness or the precipitous elements in certain of Teilhard's explanations.

However, there is no real opposition of doctrine here between them, but only a difference in what each tends to stress. Neither of them contests the point of view the other is trying to put across. Rather, each fears his own will not be appreciated by his partner at its true value.

10. See *supra,* pp. 24f., and p. 64, note 11.

11. See "Le problème de la mystique," Conclusion (*loc. cit.,* pp. 57–62); "The mystic . . . is the living and fruitful reconciliation of freedom and authority, of the most independent inner life and the most effective and disciplined social communion. . . . He is the most serene, most gentle, and most human of human beings. . . . He suffers actively and acts passively . . . And it is when he is completely alone with God that he has the most pure and effective connection to all other beings, because he finds them there, each one on its own level, in the loving will of their Creator and Saviour . . ." (pp. 61–62). Teilhard will be in complete accord with Blondel in the conviction that the highest form of activity is found in union with the *Passion.* See *supra,* p. 86, note 28.

12. See Jean Rimaud, "Vie spirituelle et philosophie, Maurice Blondel 1861–1949, *In Memoriam,*" in *Christus* (1962), pp. 272–288; pp. 281–282: Blondel "showed great understanding and sympathy for what was to become the spiritual philosophy of *The Divine Milieu,* yet maintained his own spiritual and dialectic position at the same time, orienting himself more in the voids and hollownesses of nature than in its increases and fullnesses." For Blondel's spiritual orientation, see also Henry Duméry, "La spiritualité blondelienne," in *Nouvelle revue théologique,* 1950, pp. 704–714.

7.

Teilhard de Chardin's Second Paper
to Auguste Valensin

1. Indeed, everything that Fr. Teilhard said about "the mystical milieu" and the "divine milieu" has meaning only in the context of faith. "Forma Christi" (1918), 3: "He [man] no sooner gives his consent to revealed Truth, than all the created Powers are transformed around him, as if by magic. Strange, hostile, or ambiguous until then, the natural Forces one and all are suddenly filled, *for him,* with the influence of Jesus, etc. *Credenti omnia convertuntur in Christum"* (*Ecrits,* p. 343). "L'Union créatrice" (pp. 191–192). "Mon univers" (1924; quoted in *Pensée religieuse,* p. 367, note 2). "Note sur les modes de l'action divine dans l'univers" (1920). *The Divine Milieu,* pp. 86 and 136–137, etc. And again later, in "Réflexions sur le bonheur" (lecture at Peking, December 28, 1943): "Through the persistant effort of Christian thought, the anguishing enormity of the world gradually converges overhead until it is transfigured into a center of loving energy" (*Cahiers Pierre Teilhard de Chardin,* vol. 2, 1960, p. 69). *Teilhard de Chardin, the Man and His Meaning,* pp. 169–177.

2. See "La vie cosmique": "Everything without exception, even pain and misfortune, benefit the monad of good will in the order of salvation: *Omnia cooperantur* in bonum" (*Ecrits,* p. 57). Again in "Forma Christi," 3 (p. 344): "For the Christian, a world is growing in the interior of things, a new world forming through the combined forces of faith and purpose, without

alteration of the old. A profound and simple zone is revealed to him in the heart of the universe, co-extending to all beings, a zone in which:

Quidquid patimur, Christum patimur;
Quidquid agimus, Christius agitur."

Fr. Manuel Ossa, S.J., in his thesis (in manuscript form) on *La "nouvelle naissance" d'après Maurice Blondel* (Paris, Institut Catholique, 1964) discusses the problems which Blondel and Teilhard debated; specifically, their attempts to define the relationship between the "natural transformation" and the "supernatural trans-substantiation" of the world: "Working within the restrictions of the epistolary form, Blondel did not, it seems to us, manage to express the fine points of his thinking on the problem. To understand his position, one must, we feel, follow this idea as he develops it in his dialectics, *L'Action.*" Similarly, from the same article: "The reader of this correspondence might be left with the impression that Blondel stressed the negative aspect of our relationship to the world, in contrast to the immense positive value that Teilhard attached to it. It may also seem that Blondel did not adequately justify the necessity of the rupture which, according to him, imposes on human effort the transformation effected by grace . . . (p. 1). But in reality, his philosophy leads, by "solidifying" all things in God, to giving the value of these things, and of human effort, an absolute character. The authenticity of their religious experiences meant that Blondel and Teilhard agreed on essentials; their different positions on the question of "the free act caused them to diverge in their notions of how the natural and supernatural relate, or of how all things have their substance in Christ, or again, of the value and structure of abnegation" (pp. 26–27).

Letter of December 2, 1915: "It was St. Paul who said that for those who love God, *everything* conspires to bring about the greatest good of the soul" (*The Making of a Mind*, p. 82*), etc. Hence, for the Christian who lives by faith, this is the source of the "joy of knowing that we live in the heart of a universe suranimated by our Lord" (letter of Easter, 1927). "Mon univers" (1924): ". . . When we have done our utmost to develop ourselves and to succeed, only to find that we are stopped, defeated by the forces of this world, then, *if we believe,* we discover that the power we were painfully contending with suddenly ceases to exist as a blind or evil energy. Hostile matter vanishes. And in its place, we discover the divine Master of the World who, 'under the species or appearances' of events of every sort, models us and empties us of our egoism, and penetrates into us. *'Oportet illum crescere, nos autem minui.'* This is the most magnificent prerogative of the universal Christ: the power to operate within us, not only through the natural impulses of life, but also by the terrible chaos of failure and of death."; etc. *"Diligentibus, omnia convertuntur in bonum"* (*Science et Christ,* pp. 100–101). Note on the modes of the divine action in the universe (January 1920): "For the believer, everything remains what it is for everyone else, both exteriorly and individually. And yet as God works with the whole, He adapts it with care, somehow recreating the universe at every moment, doing so expressly for the believer who prays to Him. 'Credenti, omnia convertuntur in bonum.' "

3. See "Le milieu mystique": ". . . It is done. The Fire has descended, as onto a holocaust. The mystic has now ceased to be *merely himself,* but has become, body and soul, a part of the divine. Now God passes before him for his sake, radiates His great light for his sake, as though a sacred day has been declared throughout the universe" (*Ecrits,* p. 162). *The Divine Milieu,* p. 107: "To adore . . . That means . . . to offer oneself to the fire and the transparency, to annihilate oneself in proportion to one's becoming more deliberately conscious of oneself, and to give of one's deepest to that whose depth has no end." "Mon univers" (1924: "If I never weary of pursuing creatures and perfecting them, it is only because of my hope to grasp the divine Fire which plays there within them, as in a pure crystal," —with reference to Rev. 21 (*Science et Christ,* p. 103). *"Ignem veni mittere* . . . It is not only the transformation of the earth which is desired, but also the transforming element in and of itself, the fire" (March 19, 1919). See *infra,* pp. 94–95, note 6.

4. In "Comment je vois" (1948), no. 24, Fr. Teilhard spoke out against all forms of "millenarianism."

5. At that time, he wrote in the "Note sur le progrès" (1920), humanity will have reached the "apex of its responsibility and freedom"; progress "will lead our race to a well-considered action, a fully human option" (*The Future of Man,* pp. 19 and 20). "Mon univers" (*Science et Christ,* p. 113). Other texts in *Pensée religieuse,* Ch. 10, "Evolution et liberté" (pp. 149–168). It has been suggested that if Teilhard believes in the notion of freedom, it has a rather awkward place in his "system"; but on the contrary, it is central to his thought. See "L'Hominisation" (1925): "Nothing truly existed in the universe [before the appearance of man] except a myriad of more or less obscure spontaneities. Their congested swarming gradually forced the barrier which separated the universe from freedom . . . Man, with the freedom either to lend himself to the effort or withhold himself from it, is the formidable, deadly faculty capable of measuring or criticizing life" (*La vision du passé,* pp. 103 and 106). *The Phenomenon of Man* attempts to throw some light on the "obscure and remote source of an elementary free action" taking place before the appearance of man (p. 90); he remarked that "the Mammal is already no longer completely the slave of the phylum it belongs to. Around it an 'aura' of freedom begins to float, a glimmer of personality" (pp. 155–157). *Man's Place in Nature* speaks in a similar vein of "a consciousness which in man culminates in freedom" (p. 48). Then too, in "La lutte contre la multitude," referring to the initial stage of man's development, we read that "Creation passed through a dangerous but inevitable phase . . . *Due to our freedom,* expressed in reckless or vicious acts, that which was merely a *delicate step* in the synthesis of spirit, suddenly *turned into an acute* and almost fatal *crisis*" (*Ecrits,* pp. 122–123).

As consciousness deepens, man is summoned to an ever graver option. "L'Hominisation": "In every epoch of history, each new generation has found itself in possession of a heritage enlarged by knowledge and science, in other words, faces a more conscious choice between fidelity or infidelity to life, between good and evil" (*La vision du passé,* p. 107). See "La lutte contre la multitude" (*Ecrits,* p. 132); "Mon univers" of 1924 (*Science et Christ,* p. 113); "La foi en l'homme," 1947 (t. 5, pp. 238–239), etc. *Man's Place in Nature,* p. 120: "Nothing, apparently, can prevent man-the-species from growing still greater (just as man-the-individual—for good . . . or for evil) so long as he preserves in his heart the passion for growth." There is then, in a sense, an assured progress; there is a "deep-seated and irresistible flow in the stuff of the universe" (*Man's Place in Nature*); evolution is "convergent" and "irreversible"; but the unity which is achieved can come about either through internal struggle or through harmony; this final unity can triumph in different individuals in totally different ways, according to their choices, according to their "option" for or against God ("revolt" or "adoration"), leading either to salvation or perdition.

Fr. Teilhard spoke relatively little *ex professo* of morality; at least he rarely "expressed his concept of morality in a systematic form," even though "a deep concern with morality" is almost everywhere apparent in his work. (See Denis Mermod, *La pensée morale de Teilhard de Chardin,* mimeographed thesis, Geneva, Faculté de théologie protestante, 1965.) Several times he evoked "the moral consequences of transformism" ("Les fondements et le fond de l'idée d'évolution," 1926; *La vision du passé,* pp. 185–196); he endeavored to show that evolution, in man, "becomes moral and 'mystical' " (*The Human Rebound of Evolution,* 1947; *The Future of Man,* p. 212). But for the most part his ideas on morality are approached as mystical and apologetical aspects of the problem of God and Christianity. We must also say that he tended to be overly optimistic with regard to the increase of moral freedom which is supposed to result from the growth of humanity. Still, one could hardly maintain that "evil," for Teilhard, "fades like a shadow as thought discovers its ability to extend its frontiers" (J. Chaixruy, *Demitizzazione e Morale,* Rome, 1965, p. 437). He did formulate a similar hypothesis, but it was not to become an important theme in his work. To him, says Manuel Ossa, *loc. cit.,* "the universe appeared as a function of freedom." See *The Phenomenon of Man,* p. 110: "That what is 'free' in man, can be broken down into determinisms, is no proof that the world is not based on freedom—as indeed I maintain that it is." See *Man's Place in Nature,* and *Teilhard de Chardin, the Man and His Meaning,* Ch. 13.

The "celestial Jerusalem" will contain only "chosen monads" or "elect powers": "L'Union créatrice" (*Ecrits,* pp. 195–197). Thus, a "segregation" and an "aggregation" occur simultaneously: *The Divine Milieu,* pp. 147 and 150. See letter of January 9, 1917: "For me the real earth is that chosen part of the universe, still almost universally dispersed and in course of gradual segregation, but which is little by little taking on body and form in Christ" (*The Making of a Mind,* p. 165). See "La vie cosmique" (*Ecrits,* p. 25). "La conquête du monde": ". . . movement of ascent and of segregation" (*Ecrits,* p. 67). "Les noms de la matière": "The movement which incorporates the universe into Christ is actually a segregation" (p. 429). Note of April 9, 1918: ". . . I must point out the *innervation of everything* in Christ or by Christ, AND, simultaneously, the *segregative* character of this organization." July 17, 1916: "The nebula is *in the process of segregation* and concentration around this center, around the humanity of Christ (and His mother)."

We note that this word from Teilhard's spiritual vocabulary also belonged to his scientific vocabulary. *The Phenomenon of Man,* p. 115: "The diffuse segregation of a mass within a mass?"; p. 148: "the granitic segregation of continents." *Man's Place in Nature,* "The unfolding of the biosphere and the segregation of the anthropoids." "Remarques sur les flexures continentales de Chine," in *Bulletin de la Société géologique de France,* 1946, p. 501: perhaps the continents are "large patches formed by a sialoid in the process of a gradual and continuous segregation" (quoted by Barjon and LeRoy, *La carrière scientifique de P. Teilhard de Chardin,* p. 51). Here is an example of the analogical continuity of Teilhard's concepts, evidence of the analogical continuity established between "the laws of physical chemistry and those of physical morality" ("Esquisse d'un univers personnel," in *L'Energie humaine,* p. 107).

In 1925 Blondel wrote to Fr. Valensin: "We must challenge the Origenism which tends to disregard the antitheses in, and the eternal stability of, the free option. The continuity of things does not rule out the contingency of individual solutions or the risks involved for reasoning creatures." He also expressed his wariness of "an ethical-natural determinism" (*Correspondance,* t. 3, p. 128). But in saying this, he was not really taking a stand against Teilhard's thought; he was only pointing out, as he himself said, "erorrs which one might fall into." It seems to us that the possibility of these errors dwells chiefly in the very elements of Teilhard's approach which constitutes the strength of his thought, that is, in his method as we have endeavored to define it: *La pensée religieuse,* pp. 229–247; *Teilhard de Chardin, the Man and His Meaning,* pp. 137–149.

6. Fr. Teilhard often employed the symbol of fire, particularly in *The Mass of the World* (1923) p. 21: "Fire, the source of being: we cling so tenaciously to the illusion that fire comes forth from the depths of the earth and that its flames grow progressively brighter as it pours along the radiant furrows of life's tillage. Lord, in your mercy you gave me to see that this idea is false, and that I must overthrow it if I were ever to have sight of you." "Le milieu mystique": "Lord, . . . I desire you as the Fire . . . This is the blazing universe!" (*Ecrits,* p. 148; see p. 152). "Le prêtre": "I must . . . spread the Fire that you have imparted to me" (p. 297). Letter to Fr. Valensin, May 30, 1925: "Pray that I will never allow myself to desire anything other than *the Fire!*" *The Divine Milieu,* p. 89: ". . . if the divine fire is to descend upon us." "The Spiritual Power of Matter": ". . . he whom the Lord had singled out for the road of the fire" (*Hymn of the Universe*). "The synthetic form of the Reign of God is *fire,* which assimilates *everything*" (March 20, 1919). See "Le Coeur de la matière" (1950): "Even before I went into theology, the Divine, through and under the symbol of the 'Sacred Heart,' had already taken on, for me, the form, substance, and properties of an energy, a fire."

7. Writing about matter itself, in "La vie cosmique" (1916), he had said that, "According to the Christian conception, therefore, matter retains its cosmic role, as a foundation of a lower order, nevertheless being a primordial element essential to the union; through its assimilation into the Body of Christ, something of it is destined to go into the foundations and walls of the celestial Jerusalem" (*Ecrits,* pp. 53–54). Blondel thought similarly on this point: letter to L. R., April 24, 1915 (in Blondel-Valensin, *Correspondance,* t. 3, pp. 152–154); to Henri Bremond, October 29, 1929 (in *Don Giuseppe De Luca et l'abbé Henri Bremond, 1929–1933,* Rome, 1965, p. 85), etc. See letter of January 14, 1919: "I believe . . . that one can conceive of the kingdom of God as cutting across the kingdom of man, going beyond it, integrating it, *without destroying it*" (*The Making of a Mind,* p. 279). To Fr. Fontoynont, March 15, 1916: ". . . without any rupture" (*Pensée religieuse,* p. 350). Letter (to Fr. de Lubac) of April 29, 1934: "I can keep the full essence of the drama [of human life according to Christian faith] and deepen it; but I revolt at the 'split' . . ."

8. Therefore, everything in the being is destined to be "saved," but nothing of its "form" or "shape" will remain, nothing of what he called, in his first letter, "the mean husk of all forms, all physical possession" (see *supra,* p. 29). See "Mon univers" (1924): The world must "lose its visible form, both in us and in its totality"; it "can only reach God *in Christo Jesu* through a total recasting, during which it will seem to be utterly defeated *without any applicable compensations* (of a terrestrial kind)" (*Science et Christ,* p. 102). See *La pensée religieuse,* Ch. 12, "Transfiguration du Cosmos." *The Divine Milieu,* p. 99, n. 2: "The fire of heaven must come down on something: otherwise there would be nothing consumed and nothing consummated." This can be compared with *Paul Claudel interroge le Cantique des cantiques* (1948), pp. 356–357: "I am the prey for someone who needs everything that is mortal in me for the purposes of making the immortal; of everything that is human in me to pitilessly turn it into God! . . . Consume, consummate! *Consumo, consummo! . . .*"

110

9. Ralph Waldo Emerson (1803–1882), widely read even in the first quarter of the twentieth century. He extolled an "ideal Church," outside of all "form"; for him Jesus was a "genius as a moral educator" and he denied Him any "mystical role." He exalted a "moral sense" surpassing all great men who transmit it, and reduced all religion to morality. Fr. Louis Bouyer wrote that "all Christian and biblical reality was vaporized" in his "transcendentalism"; see *The Spirit and Forms of Protestantism* (Westminster, 1956).

10. See *The Phenomenon of Man*, Preface, p. 29: ". . . have marked the places . . . for breaches, etc." The exact meaning of these reflections is given in the Teilhardian doctrine of analogy: our views must undergo "an essential correction each time we attempt to follow any line of reality through a new sphere of the universe. The world is metamorphosed from sphere to sphere, is enriched and internally recast. And consequently it appears each time in a new state, one in which all of its earlier properties are partially retained, partially renewed": "Le phénomène humain," 1928 (*Science et Christ*, p. 122); this is described analogically as a succession of "thresholds" and "critical points." *Ibid.*, pp. 126–127: if we accept his concept of the phenomenon of man, "we will find ourselves in possession of a key which (if we orient ourselves in the right analogies) will enable us to explore the universe from the inside, while physics up to now has tried to grasp it from the outside." See also "Note sur le Christ universel" (January, 1920): "Since union in Christ is formed between people, these [social] analogies are true. But they are incomplete. To grasp the whole truth, we must correct them by analogies taken from strictly natural and physical realities" (*Science et Christ*, p. 43). "La maîtrise du monde et le règne de Dieu" (*Ecrits*, pp. 75–76). Note on " 'L'Elément universel' du monde": ". . . in accordance with what Scholasticism has to say about *the analogy of being*" (p. 362). It therefore concerns a mental operation that Teilhard carefully distinguished from the "metaphor" or from extrinsic analogies; objective analogies "which correspond . . . to a deep bond of nature" (*The Phenomenon of Man*, p. 116). See *Teilhard de*

111

Chardin, the Man and His Meaning, pp. 169–177. Emile Rideau, *La pensée du Père Teilhard de Chardin* (Paris, 1965), p. 52: "The concept of an 'analogy,' or of correspondence, played a vital role in Teilhard's thought. As he looked into the depths of being, he saw it constructed as a network of unified planes; this is a profoundly human conception, and the essence of knowledge, poetry, and religion."

11. See "Le milieu mystique": "I perceive that all perfection, even that which is natural, is the necessary basis for the mystical and definitive organism that you are constructing by means of all things. You do not destroy the beings which you take unto yourself, Lord, but transform them by consummating all the good that centuries of creation have evolved in them."

12. See *supra,* p. 109, note 6. "Le milieu mystique": "The Fire which descends" (*Ecrits,* pp. 161–162). See letter from Peking, to R. H., September 21, 1929: ". . . You seem to be saying: The Christian ought to make the world beautiful in order to have something more beautiful to *let go of,* through his love of God. (I exaggerate, but on purpose.) Therefore, in speaking of the holocaust, in speaking of the world that is sacrificed to God, you lay stress on that portion of it which *goes up in smoke* (in other words, your prime concern is the *transcendence* of God, as was Blondel's when I knew him eight years ago). Personally, I tend to stress the other side of it—(in any case, you should give a clearer picture of its complementary role). The Christian, I like to think, should make the world beautiful and push it to its extremes because there is an *opus* maturing within it, one which, purified by death, will be *integrated* into the Pleroma. I am particularly drawn to the idea that during the holocaust, the elements are not *consumed* but *consummated* by the divine fire (one does not exclude the other, moreover—in fact, to the contrary!). In this sense, you approach the solution through the notion of a 'preference' (stressing abandonment and the relinquishing of things), whereas I approach it through the notion of an 'excentration' (the things which man has conquered always stay with him, through some subtle essence of themselves—but their *center* shifts). The

Christian somehow carries his definitive *I* over into a sort of super-person: Christ—and he enlarges (or destroys) his egoism, rather than becoming disinterested in his work. Herein lies the essence of Christianity, as I see it: to take a universe which tended to be centered upon itself and to excentrate it over to God. Isn't this one of the profound facets of the Incarnation-Redemption? Before God and world could fuse in the pleroma, it was necessary that God somehow *break out of His sphere* to take our imperfections into Himself and transfigure them: this is the passion; and at the same time we must be fit to be drawn into the superior *sphere* which attracts us: this is our death and mortification." *The Divine Milieu,* p. 73: "When He [the Master of Death] enters into us to destroy, as it seems, the virtues and the forces that we have distilled with so much loving care out of the sap of the world, it will be as a loving fire to consummate our completion in union."

13. See *supra,* p. 68, note 11. The original meaning of "Omega" in Teilhard's thought was therefore "our Lord Jesus Christ" or "the fullness of Christ." Thus, it was first of all a religious symbol, borrowed from the Apocalypse, and was expanded in meaning as Teilhard assimilated the writings of St. Paul. The scientific symbolism and the phenomenological meaning came later.

14. On the mystery of damnation: *The Divine Milieu,* pp. 146–149, "The outer darkness and the lost souls." Earlier, he wrote in "La vie cosmique" (1916), ch. 4: ". . . He is not surprised to find that here, as elsewhere, a hell is the natural corollary of heaven, and he learns to dread it" (*Ecrits,* pp. 57–58). "Christ in the World of Matter," in *Hymn of the Universe.* "La lutte contre la multitude" (1927): ". . . In the heart of his immortal substance, the damned undergoes the conscious horrors of an eternal decomposition." "Forma Christi" (1918), 5 (*Ecrits,* pp. 100–101, 132, 349–350). *The Mass of the World* (1923): ". . . Even those who find themselves cast outside of your love, continue to receive the support of your presence, but to their misery." See "Mon univers" (1924), on the second coming: ". . . The angelic trumpets are only a weak symbol.

The monads, stirred by the most powerful organic attraction imaginable (the very force of cohesion of the universe), will be precipitated to the point where the total maturation of things and the implacable irreversibility of the entire history of the world will irrevocably destine them—some, of spiritualized matter, to the boundless conclusion of an eternal Communion, —others, of materialized spirit, to the conscious horrors of an interminable decomposition" (*Science et Christ,* p. 113). Equally significant is the prayer which ends the paragraph on "the outer darkness" in *The Divine Milieu.*

Here again it seems quite clear that Fr. Teilhard has drawn support from Maurice Blondel, not for the upholding of the dogma certainly, but in his way of expressing it, and in the place he gives Blondel in the presentation of his thought. See *L'Action* (1893), pp. 359–373: "The Death of Action." J. Wehrlé, "une soutenance de thèse," in *Annales de philosophie chrétienne,* May, 1907, pp. 26–30 (discussion between Blondel and Gabriel Séailles). See also Blondel's "Principe élémentaire d'une logique de la vie morale," in vol. 2 of the *Premier Congrès international de philosophie* (Paris, 1900). See letter to Fr. Auguste Valensin, November 20, 1913, on the objectivity of knowledge, "a preparatory passage for a more complete realism with regard to the debt incurred by ἕξις or στέοησις" (*Correspondance,* t. 3, p. 52). On the subject of "option" in Blondel's philosophy: Albert Cartier, *Existence et Vérité, Philosophie blondélienne de l'Action et Problématique existentielle* (1955), especially pp. 235–248: "The poor choice leads to the isolation of existence. The good choice leads to the universalization of existence." Hans Urs von Balthasar has treated this question on several occasions, and with a depth of insight unequaled in our times; see, for example, "Christian Universalism," in *Word and Redemption* (New York, 1965), pp. 127–145. See *supra,* p. 106, note 5.

15. See pp. 217–219 in *Ecrits,* the Preface to "L'Ame du monde."

16. "La vie cosmique," ch. 3: "New life. . . , the unforeseen increases and 'dutiful' extension of our natural capacities"

(*Ecrits*, p. 40). Compare with Saint Thomas Aquinas, *De veritate*, q. 27, art. 6, ad 1: "*Gratia perficit naturam*"; *In Boetium de Trinitate*, q. 2, art. 3: "*Natura praeambula est ad gratiam*"; "*Dona gratiarum hoc modo naturae adduntur, quod eam non tollunt, sed magis perficiunt*"; *Summa Theologica*, I, I, q. 1, art. 8, ad 2; I, II, q. 3, art. 8, etc. See Etienne Gilson, *The Spirit of Thomism* (New York, 1964): "Thomism extends the natural through the supernatural." A. Lemonnyer, O.P., in St. Thomas, *La vie humaine, ses formes, ses états* (II, II, q. 179–189), p. 500: St. Thomas "holds that there is a connection and a close parallelism" between nature and grace (Edition of *La revue des jeunes*, 1926). Guy de Broglie, S.J., *Autour de la notion thomiste de la béatitude*, Archives de philosophie, vol. 3 (1925), p. 222, note: St. Thomas shows how charity "brings nature to a completion which lies in a direction already roughly indicated by its active inclinations." We know, for example, that for St. Thomas the first natural love, far from being comparable to an egoistical desire, is practically a beginning of charity: charity develops "not to destroy a thing, but to complete it" (I, q. 60, art. 5). It could have been said of him that he was not satisfied with proving that "at best, and under duress, a Greek could manage to adapt himself to Christianity"; he wanted to establish that Christianity alone "could fully guarantee his ideal, and afford him its complete realization": Etienne Gilson, quoted by Dom A. Stolz, *Théologie de la mystique* (Paris, 1939), p. 156. This was precisely Teilhard's position with respect to the man of science, and in a deeper sense, with respect to the "natural" world. This continuity which St. Thomas saw in the two orders does not rule out our recognizing the transcendence and heterogeneity of grace: see J.-B. Beumer, S.J., "*Gratia supponit naturam*, Zur Geschichte eines theologischen Prinzips," in *Gregorianum*, 20 (1939), pp. 381–406; Erich Przywara, S.J., "Der Grundsatz *Gratia non destruit sed supponit et perficit naturam*," in *Scholastik* (1942, 2), pp. 178–186. Likewise for Teilhard, by "extending" nature, grace "transforms" and "folds it upon itself." See again Olivier Rabut, O.P., *Teilhard de Chardin* (New York, 1961). N. M. Wildiers, *Teilhard de*

Chardin (1960), pp. 102 and 114. See footnote in *The Phenomenon of Man,* p. 298; or *The Divine Milieu:* "The noble path of the Cross is none other than the path of human effort, supernaturally corrected and extended."

17. See Karl Rahner, S.J., "Current Problems in Christology," in *Theological Investigations,* vol. 1 (Baltimore and London, 1961), pp. 165, 167: ". . . we must remember that the world is something in which everything is related to everything else, and that consequently anyone who makes some portion of it into his own history, takes for himself the world as a whole for his personal environment. Consequently it is not pure fantasy (although the attempt must be made with caution) to conceive of the 'evolution' of the world *towards Christ,* and to show how there is a gradual ascent which reaches a peak in him. Only we must reject the idea that this 'evolution' could be a striving upward of what is below by its own powers. If Col. 1, 15, is true, and is not attenuated in a moralistic sense; if then in Christ the world as a whole, even in its 'physical' reality, has really reached historically through Christ that point in which God becomes all in all, then an attempt like this cannot be false in principle. . . . The Christ would appear as the summit of this history and Christology as its sharpest formulation, . . ."

18. Another instance of the substantial agreement between the two parties. Each recognizes in principle that the other's point of view is well-founded, but each believes it necessary to stress a different point, and explains his reasons for doing so. Both fear that the other might not value these reasons at their due, or at least, might overlook them; this leads to a rather notable divergence of orientation in the whole of their respective thought. See p. 101, note 9.

19. This is the dialectic explained earlier, p. 33 (see p. 83, note 17) and p. 35.

20. See *supra,* pp. 111–112, notes 10 and 11.

21. This is the title of an essay that he had just written at Jersey while in the company of Fr. Auguste Valensin, July and August, 1919: "The Spiritual Power of Matter" (*Ecrits,* pp. 433–446; also *Hymn of the Universe*). Letter of August 8:

". . . I'm fairly pleased with it, because I feel that I got across what I was putting into words. But it will hardly be intelligible to anyone who isn't already familiar from another source with my views of the role and nature of matter. Others, who haven't been prepared for it, will take me for some sort of rebel" (*The Making of a Mind,* p. 300). To gain a better understanding of this essay, one would do well to refer to the essay on "Les noms de la matière," written not long before it (Easter, 1919; *Ecrits,* pp. 415–432). And to avoid several gross errors in interpretation, one should always bear in mind that here, as elsewhere, the person speaking is a believer who expresses himself through faith, who sees matter as an "ocean agitated by spirit," a "clay moulded and animated by the incarnate Word," and who looks to it for "effort, separation, and death."

The term was also to become a title to one of the sub-sections of *The Divine Milieu,* pp. 81–87; see p. 84, for the distinction between "matter *taken in the material and carnal sense*" and "matter *taken in the spiritual sense.*" On the subject of matter and spirit, one might also, for example, refer to "Science et Christ, ou analyse et synthèse" (1921), 1 (*Science et Christ,* pp. 48–57): ". . . He who knows how to see, finds in the analysis of matter the priority and primacy of spirit" (p. 57). "L'Union créatrice" (*Ecrits,* pp. 178–179). In "Mon univers" (1924), Fr. Teilhard explains "this principle that 'spirit is the source of all substance' . . . Things are held together solely by an effort of synthesis, in short, by a reflection of spirit" . . . "Everything is held from above . . . First, this principle consecrates the sovereignty of spirit. But it saves and ennobles matter at the same time, etc." (*Science et Christ,* pp. 77–81.) "Le phénomène spirituel" (1937), Conclusion: "The problem which troubles our intelligence is this, that the world manifests opposed but associated elements (spirit and matter) in a chain of combinations, a chain flung out on a trajectory, possessing duration, steering a course between thought and the unconscious" (*L'Energie humaine*); "The phenomenon of spirit . . . is the cosmic movement par excellence, —everything is suspended from it and nothing can explain it" (*ibid.,* p. 123). "Du cosmos à la cosmogénèse" (*L'Activation de l'énergie,* p. 267). "Les singularités de l'espèce humaine," p. 48; etc. See Paul Grenet, *Pierre Teilhard de Chardin* (New York and London, 1966), p. 69: "Let there be no mistake, Teilhard never loved Matter for its own sake but only for the purpose it was serving . . . That which moves in the heart of Matter, which is born in the Flesh and dies in the Flesh, all this was only a point of departure for Teilhard . . ." (with quotations from *The Mass of the World*). See *supra,* p. 29.

22. See letter to Marguerite Teillard, from Docelles (Vosges), November 13, 1918: "What you tell me in your letter of the 7th, of the increasing importance that the idea of sacrifice is taking on for you, has been a great joy to me, because I think that this shows that you are making your way into the final circle of divine union, and that you are doing so after having been through the circle of human attractions, and have thereby strengthened both your power to give and your capacity to achieve detachment. For those in whose eyes God has become the supreme reality in the universe, there can logically be no more stable and more profound happiness than to feel this reality painfully taking the place of their own being—insofar as that being has been faithful in shaping and developing itself. It's an ultimate happiness that nobody can appreciate who has not been the object of this precious transformation" (*The Making of a Mind,* p. 251). See "L'Atomisme de l'esprit" (1941), in *L'Activation de l'énergie,* p. 63. The same doctrine was formulated by Jules Monchanin, *Ecrits spirituels,* with an Introduction by Edouard Duperray (Paris, 1965), p. 121: "Is it true that 'in renouncing the world, a man is thereby enabled to understand it'? . . . It all depends on the quality of his renunciation . . . And above all, on the reason why he renounces . . . One should only renounce things that one has attained (one has to reach a thing first before he can go beyond it); a fullness, in view of a still greater fullness . . ."

23. See "Mon univers" (1918): "I hope . . . with all my strength that the elements of truth concerning action and universal presence of God and Christ, as universally believed and

professed by the Church, will be ultimately considered, together and without attenuation." To Marguerite Teillard, October 15, 1916: "You feel . . . how complicated these questions are and how they need to be treated in conformity with the spirit and living tradition of the Church" (*The Making of a Mind,* p. 132). *The Divine Milieu,* p. 86, appeals to "the constant attitude and practical teaching of the Church with regard to human suffering."

24. See letter from Jersey, August 21, 1919; writing of his friend Fr. Charles, he said: "We agreed to keep in touch regularly. And then, as I'd long been thinking, we decided that the best way to spread our views was to start, first of all, from theology, from scripture, from the Church's mystical practice. That's the basic foundation, the firmest, which all the philosophies can do no more than illustrate, with more or less accuracy" (*The Making of a Mind,* p. 302). See "L'Atomisme de l'esprit" (1941): ". . . the immutable axis of sainthood" (*L'Activation de l'énergie,* p. 63). To the very degree that the solutions outlined by Fr. Teilhard are unable to satisfy us, we will still have to follow his advice, upheld by his constant example: "It is time, in all branches of mystical science, to examine by study and prayer that area where God and the Cosmos meet and touch" ("Note pour l'évangélisation des temps nouveaux," in *Ecrits,* p. 377).

25. Fr. Teilhard strove to do this throughout his life. It can be sensed most strongly in the notes he wrote during his retreats. Establishing that "his particular area [one which he assigned himself and which he was to cultivate steadily from that point on] was the passion of Omega, of Omegalization, and the making known and dissemination of Omega," he told himself again and again that he should not go about it through words alone, but through the way he lived (and died): "Jesus, teach me the action which reveals Omega!", etc. (retreats of 1940 *ss.*).

26. Fr. Teilhard often asked others for their opinion and criticism, just as he has done here with Maurice Blondel. He also wrote a number of short personal essays to "lighten the task of criticism and reorientation for those whose right it is to guide me" (1918). "My one wish is to be advised" (1933), etc.

Similar texts are found in *Pensée religieuse,* pp. 18–20, and in *Teilhard de Chardin, the Man and His Meaning.*

On February 15, 1955, writing from New York to Claude Cuénot, Teilhard said of Blondel: "I owe him a great deal. But ultimately we do not see eye to eye." He regretted a "certain absence of the 'cosmic sense' " in Blondel; —this is not entirely fair, and indicates a certain failing of memory; he also denies him a real feeling for "a universe in the state of cosmogenesis"; —this has more truth to it, and amounts to saying that Blondel was not Teilhard. (See Claude Cuénot, "Situation de Teilhard de Chardin," in the *Bulletin industriel de Mulhouse,* 1963). Moreover, Fr. Teilhard may not have had a very clear recollection of this exchange of papers. One might compare this with what he said about Newman, in another letter to Claude Cuénot, May 21, 1953: "During the first war, I read a little of Newman (*The Grammar of Assent*) with pleasure. But I was not conscious of his having made a strong impression on me." (*loc. cit.*) However, in his letters from that period he spoke of reading Newman's *Apologia* and from the way he praised it, we gather that he derived something more than pleasure from it. Letter to Fr. Victor Fontoynont, March 15, 1916: ". . . Through necessity and choice I have reapplied myself to thought and prayer, now and then inspired by one of these books (the only sort a person should write) in which a life is laid bare, Newman's *Apologia* or *The Dream of Gerontius*" (quoted in *Pensée religieuse,* p. 348). See letter to Marguerite Teillard, February 2, 1916: "I haven't yet finished Newman's *Apologia,* etc."; July 22, 1916: "To counter the boredom of the trenches I've been reading Thureau-Dangin's *Newman Catholique,* which Guiguite [his sister Marguerite-Marie] sent me. I feel more than ever in sympathy with the great Cardinal, so undaunted, so firm of faith, so full, as he says himself, 'of life and thought,' —and at the same time, so thwarted. And once again I was conscious within myself of the inspiration that calls me to the great work of reconciling the supreme and absolute love of God with the lower (but still legitimate and necessary) love of life embraced under its natural forms. —A host of Newman's ideas . . . so far-reaching, so open, and hence realistic, have entered into my mind as into a dwelling long familiar to them. And what has made it all the more heartening to me to find this community of inclination and appreciation, is that the man who felt them so deeply had bitterly experienced, without being scandalized, the bitter temptation of being born before the due hour or season of his thought." December 5, 1916: "Somewhere in his *Apologia* Newman says 'He and I' as he recalls a strong feeling he had at a particular moment, a sense of the only two essentials in direct confrontation—those which contain all the rest between them and which, together, sum it up. May you feel this fundamental and peace-bringing simplification of the world quickening within you." And January 9, 1917 (*The Making of a Mind,* pp. 93, 114, 148*). In 1916 he also read, or reread, the *Essay on the Development of Christian Doctrine:* this book "was born out of the needs of his inner life; he discusses the solution to the religious (and total [?]) problem as it arose in his life. I feel that I should write (at least for myself) something similar, avoiding, as he did, the task which is proper to the Church (the attempt to reconcile antiquity with "innovation'), and dealing with the cosmic Becoming (the attempt to reconcile detachment with the legitimate love of γήμητηε)" (February 28). "The more I read Newman, the more I feel a kinship (undoubtedly a humble one) between his mind and mine. And one of the fruits of this is the stimulation I receive from his example, the impetus to finish *my* work" (July 17). On visiting Oxford, he wrote to his parents, on October 8, 1911: "I was particularly drawn to St. Mary's, due to associations with Cramner and Newman . . ." He read the following thought in Newman, and it held great meaning for him throughout his life: "Those who try to win the day for a truth, *before its time,* run the risk of ending as heretics" (*The Making of a Mind,* p. 114). An essay on "Pascal, Newman, and Teilhard de Chardin," by Dr. Iso Baumer, was published in *Orientierung* (September, 1962), pp. 204–208.

27. On January 10, 1920, Fr. Teilhard wrote from Paris to Fr. Auguste Valensin, then at Aix: "Yesterday I received a

letter from Maurice Blondel. He mentions your visits, how much good they do him, and how much they mean to him." But this letter, it seems, was not a continuation of their discussion; in any case, Fr. Teilhard says nothing about it. What he does say is that he has received "some lengthy and perceptive reflections from Fr. Maréchal, concerning several papers of mine which Fr. Charles had sent him. —He goes along with me on quite a number of things concerning evolution (especially biological evolution) and on the desiderata of current philosophy. But he hangs back when it comes to the main points . . . I feel that Father Maréchal's philosophy is still far too separated from his theology and mysticism—and also that the concessions he makes to the unity of development of the universe should logically take him much further than he actually goes." Fr. Joseph Maréchal was a professor of philosophy at the Jesuit college in Louvain.

In 1925 Fr. Valensin had Blondel read the second of Teilhard's essays bearing the title "Mon Univers" (1924). We find Blondel's response, dated September 12, 1925, in Blondel-Valensin, *Correspondance,* t. 3 (1965), pp. 126–130. It echoes his letters of 1919, pointing out that he is sympathetically disposed towards Teilhard's stance, and expressing the same reservations he had had earlier. If Teilhard replied, his letter has not been found.

Fr. Teilhard remembered Blondel until the end. On February 8, 1955, writing to Mgr. Bruno de Solages about his great "spiritual energetics" project, he remarked, "An energetics singularly related to the Blondelian metaphysics of *L'Action . . .*"

The Aims and Scope of the Work of Teilhard de Chardin

M. Georges Gusdorf has recently published a most stimulating book entitled *L'Université en question*. A thought-provoking work, it opens with a brief historical survey, somewhat condensed, perforce simplified, where the author, wc cannot help remarking, takes the Jesuits to task in a way which we consider unwarranted (for example, he does not seem to be aware of the efforts of a certain Maldonat to modernize the Sorbonne in 16th-century Paris). There follows a description—rather smacking of caricature, we feel—of the problems and struggles of the French "university" today. For us, the book's value lies mainly in the author's thoughtful assessment of modern culture, particularly in his warning that it may perish in the hands of an ever-growing, unprecedented specialization.

"The epistemological frontiers," says M. Gusdorf, "have become airtight, rigorously asepticized compartments. Intelligence and imagination seem to suffocate outside them. Everybody believes himself to be the master of a heritage which he must jealously guard from outsiders. . . . This leads to a general crumbling of knowledge, and is very costly to the state of high culture . . ."[1]

How true this is, at least of a great many areas. But unfortunately the malady is always easier to find than the cure. We look to Fr. Teilhard de Chardin's thought-system as a possible source of help in our attempt to put a stop to this crumbling. For he was distressed about it and opposed it in his work.

If we could point to any one grievance shared by Fr. Teilhard's adversaries these last ten years, it would be the complaint that he confuses and jumbles different systems of thought. But the more closely one studies his work, the more one realizes that he was extremely careful to distinguish one from another the individual contributions coming from diverse sources of knowledge, and that he respected the diversity of methods required by the different disciplines of mind. If he found analogies between them, it was never through oversimplification. One admits to having simply skimmed through his writings if one says, for example, that he gave his faith in Christ an unwarranted place in a system which set out to be scientific and which called itself such. He never confused "the truth evolving here on earth" with "the truth descended from heaven,"[2] but rather, recognized the qualities and content particular to each, as well as their different origins; he did, however, hope to show that they must end up "joining each other" without losing their respective natures. He took a stand against attempts at reconciliation which "lump together the aims and sources of knowledge" and inescapably lead to "arrangements without stability, in that they are unnatural." Before accusing him of "concordism," therefore, one ought at least to read what he has to say on the subject.[3] Another very real error is to claim, as has been done, that he ruined Christian faith by trying to give it its groundwork within a system. Did St. Thomas Aquinas ruin Christian faith by trying to prove the existence of God and the immortality of the soul, or by believing, through faith, in the permanent establishment of a new heaven and earth?[4] One could ask the same of all the authentic representatives of Christian philosophy at any point in history.

Still, it is true that Fr. Teilhard's great aim was synthesis, to achieve "coherence" and "totality" at one and the same time. Just as he wanted no confusion of the different "meridians" of the "mental sphere" "at the equator," he felt that "they must converge somewhere at a pole of collective vision. Otherwise, everything in the domain of thought and knowledge would collapse." Then too, he saw "true scientific progress" as an "uncovering of the underlying relationships which draw together areas heretofore quite unrelated to our eye." And he felt that "a theory's value is reflected in the increase in order it brings to our vision of the world" and that to reach a real understanding of something, one should "approach it from different angles, and on different levels," ever attentive, however, to the "converging" lines which draw it to its final unity.[5] In 1924 he wrote in "Mon Univers," "My one great desire is to show how one can approach the immense disorder of things from a certain direction and suddenly find their obscurity and discord passing into an ineffable vibration, inexhaustibly rich in note and nuance, utterly perfect in its unity." And in the same vein, in 1934, "The more I think about it, the more convinced I am that the sole criterion of truth is whether or not the concept in question can offer us a peak increase in universal coherence. Such an attainment has an objective quality about it, transcending the effects of the personality." Then in 1936, he wrote, "*Truth* is nothing but the total coherence of the universe relating to every point of itself."[6] He did not waver in his belief that the best criterion lay in whether one could point to positive results in one's quest for points of convergence, because "truth alone can bring about an effortless synthesis of reality."[7]

A number of people have been quick to find fault with Teilhard's way of beginning with science and going on into metaphysics, or of going from the natural realm of science and reason into the supernatural realm of Christian faith, or again, of going from the realm of the supernatural into the realm of creation. To them, these moves are just so many paralogisms. We do not say *a priori* that his work is beyond criticism on this point. In his desire to shed light on the "remarkable similarity" between the "views of dogmatics" and what we learn in studying the "phenomenon of man,"[8] it is true that he does allow himself a number of short cuts which may be confusing to a reader who is not able to see them against the context of his work as a whole. At times he may have failed to give a clear explanation of the analogical nature of his vocabulary. Then too, speaking of two systems, he was more apt to indicate where they merged than where they parted ways—a tendency responsible, nevertheless, for the most original and fertile elements in his approach. His adversaries have accused him of "transgression" on three counts; these protests, it seems to us, stem from the very prejudices and short-sightedness which M. Gusdorf so understandably complains of in one of his earlier works, a short-sightedness where "each discipline resists encroachment upon itself." He sees Fr. Teilhard as sternly opposing this tendency and calls him "the greatest name in French anthropology since Broca."[9]

This sterile, static compartmentalization of the sciences is found in scholarly abstractions and work routines within the professions. Fr. Teilhard de Chardin discovered that physics and biology—we might say the science of matter and the science of life—stood in a complementary relationship to one another, and were indispensable to each other as such. Yet he did not go so far as to group them into one discipline. Well aware of the complexity of reality, he spoke of "several physics" and several biologies[10] and urged others to do so too. Likewise, in 1923, he maintained that anatomy and morphology have "emptied the phenomenon of man of its specific properties, for they have worked in an area where they could not help but mutilate human value with their narrow methods."[11] And in 1930 he asked, "Aren't the equations of mechanics turning out to be closely related to those of light? What would have become of modern physics if radioactivity had been simply set aside as an irksome, bizarre phenomenon?"[12] The main point here is this—that "thinking Man is generally regarded as an 'irregular feature' of the universe. But he represents a privileged phenomenon where one of the most general aspects of the cosmos is placed before our eyes, placed before us in such brilliance that man is known right away for what he is."[13]

The same can be said, *mutatis mutandis,* of the ties between philosophy and the sciences. Despite the frequent objections raised on both sides, one cannot fail to see, without misconstruing history, that advances in scientific thinking have had their influence on the development of philosophy, and that conversely, "philosophical thought has had its influence on the evolution of scientific theories."[14] The even sharper distinction drawn between knowledge of the world we live in, on the one hand, originating in man, and the truth of faith, on the other, originating in divine revelation, does not mean that here too, fruitful ties cannot be established, bridging the gap. Where, then, do we encounter the refusal to allow the attitude of faith to illuminate the entire universe? Not in the great works of the Catholic tradition; but in decadent theology alone, which "operates in an area of thought which most moderns have deserted," thus abandoning the traditional nobility of its role without even realizing it is doing so; it allows itself to become a narrow specialty, nothing more, a process in a vacuum jar or in an outlying area where the intellect ceases to function.

Fr. Teilhard de Chardin was well aware of the fact that analytical science does not, in and of itself, lead one to Christian faith, nor even towards a simple affirmation of God. Indeed, he was as fully aware of this as were those who felt they had to remind him of it. He spoke to this matter with great clarity. "When the mind wants to know what a given thing consists of, its first step is to take the thing apart, to analyze it. The whole of science stems from this instinctive act." And it has been eminently successful. "Things revealed their nature with an astonishing lack of resistance." But so far, this success is only a practical one, for an act of this kind "reduces everything in turn to a swarming of elements, these elements guided by nothing but statistical laws of great quantities and chance." In short, living beings are pulverized by analytical science. Is it surprising, then, that "the analytic observation of phenomena [is] incapable of bringing us into touch with God?" Such a process drags our thinking down further and further "to the very lowest planes of reality," to the dreary regions of plurality and unconsciousness. Clearly, every being is a synthesis. Really to learn something about it, we should begin by turning a critical eye on the analytical approach we originally started with (without rejecting any of the valuable information it afforded us). "Do we not judge the perfection of an animal, or the supremacy of the thinking being, by the penetration and synthetic power of its gaze?"[15] We should ask ourselves whether there is a change ahead, a change Fr. Teilhard felt sure was taking place. "Modern thought," he wrote, "was once excessively prone to the charms of analysis, to the point of falling into illusion"; now, however, it is beginning to reaccustom itself to "the evolutively creative function of synthesis"; for "there is decidedly *more* in the molecule than in the atom, *more* in the cell than in the molecule, *more* in society than in the individual, *more* in mathematical constructions than in calculations and theorems. . . . At each further stage in the process of combining, *something emerges* into a new order, and this *something* cannot be traced to the isolated elements involved or to their sum."[16] In short, "reality's principal movement is a synthesis" and physics ought to go on to become a "hyper-physics" or an "ultra-physics" recognizing this "law of universal structure." In that way we will begin to see that the only real substance and the only real originality possible are those which have been given to a being by its ability to "synthesize"; for it is true that "everything," from the individual creature to the universe as a whole, "is held from above"—or what amounts to the same thing, held by a "tilting forward." Thus, whatever the reality one may be studying, one finds himself constrained to proceed "step by step" "to the very end of the world"—that is, to climb from one degree to the next to the final Principle of all being.[17]

This, then, is what lies at the core of Fr. Teilhard's "phenomenology." Synthesis becomes a follow-up step to analysis. Thus, his phenomenology enables him to move from a being's "without" to its "within" and clears the way for conducting metaphysical inquiry into what is considered "positive" science. In his study of evolution it allows him, first of all, to trace the spread of the physio-chemical laws and the physio-moral laws without confusing their phases or areas of application. And in taking him "beyond the classical bounds of science, it proves to be a major contribution to the methodology of the contemplation of the world."[18] And finally, when Christian dogmatics, coming forward from another quarter, was to afford him both the strengthening and the complementary viewpoint which enabled him to escape the vertigo of appearances and to contemplate the universe, here again he was to find, beyond the "question of one particular school of thought over another," the movement of theological syntheses of the past.[19]

* * *

We might here examine a text dating from an early period. Though it speaks only to the relationship between "religion" and "evolution," Teilhard felt that its general meaning was applicable to all similar relationships.

"It is evident that *the time has finally come* to regather the disjointed fragments, to reunite the complementary qualities, to put the vertex of the pyramid back on its base. Religion and evolution should neither be confused nor separated; they are destined to form a single unbroken organism, their respective lives furthering each other, supporting each other, fulfilling each other reciprocally, neither identifying with one another nor destroying one another, the one presenting an infinite ideal and immutable laws, the other furnishing a seat of activity and the material necessary to the changing of beings in growth. Since duality is manifest in our time, our task is to synthesize it!"[20]

He summed up this view in the chapter heading "Harmony," and referred to it elsewhere, in a more subjective and practical frame of mind, as "the alliance of the passion of the world and the passion of God."[21]

One can certainly debate the successes and failures of such an undertaking. And one may well find shortcomings in the way the Teilhardian objective was pursued. We have done so ourselves, on a number of occasions. One may share Fr. Edouard Boné's view that "the effort to synthesize scientific phenomenology and Christian thought ought to be carried forward by qualified thinkers, philosophers, and theologians. These men should go back over the road, following its general and hastily erected markers, and verify the value of each discovery."[22] This was a wish often expressed by Fr. Teilhard himself. But here again advocates of a certain point of view in both the Catholic and Protestant[23] Churches have attacked *the principle* underlying his effort, and we consider this attack untenable. For through Teilhard, this contention of principles tends to smother any enterprise which might try to bring about the Teilhardian aim, an aim whose legitimacy is above question. To contest it, all affirmation of the "cosmic role" of Christ is brushed aside, and this would be most regrettable.[24] Has not a certain theologian turned a deaf ear to the best exegetes of the epistles of St. Paul and imagined he might refute Teilhard by declaring that the humanity of Christ exercises no influence on the substance and evolution of the world? Has it not been further maintained, through an appeal to the authority of this theologian, that "this is invincible from the Catholic point of view" and that "a statement to the contrary is a departure from Catholicism?"[25] Equally regrettable is the refusal to admit Fr. Teilhard's conviction that the Christ of the revelation is none other than the "Omega" he was led to postulate through pondering cosmic evolution. By this point Teilhard was hardly claiming, as seems to be believed, that our knowledge of Christ, as revealed by supernatural means, does not go expressly beyond our knowledge of Omega as sensed or established by natural means; in fact, he maintains the very opposite. Rather, here is what we feel would be catastrophic—to take issue with Teilhard, to find oneself adopting the position that the Revealed of the divine revelation and the Ultimate of rational knowledge are not one and the same, but are irreparably distinct—just as catastrophic as if we considered ourselves pledged to believe that the God of philosophy (neither we nor Teilhard use Pascal's term "the God of philosophers and servants") were actually distinct from the "God of Jesus Christ."[26]

Although Fr. Teilhard was interested in science from an early age, he did not devote himself to research until relatively late in life. He did not dedicate himself to it with real seriousness until he had finished his theological studies, and even then he did not finish his doctor's thesis until after the First World War, at the age of forty. In all likelihood, his natural impulse towards unity and his need for consistency and the absolute would not, in and of themselves, have been sufficient to see him through, or even make a good start in, this work of total synthesis, his first love. For this, we should look to his training in the Society of Jesus, at the theological colleges at Hastings and Jersey. Here, part of the curriculum was purely religious, but another, a considerable and indispensable part, consisted of intensive training in literature, philosophy, and theology. Lately, certain gaps have been noted in this training, certain shortcomings, chiefly those which would explain a few of his extreme reactions and the incompleteness of a number of his views. All the remarks made on this subject are not equally correct. Nevertheless, those which are true should not keep us from recognizing that this training was of immense value to his genius, affording him a thorough exposure to disciplines which were to enrich his thought throughout his life. He spoke of this himself and in terms, it seems to us, of highest praise. "The marvelous training I received at the Society," he wrote to his friend Auguste Valensin, "ended by making me desire one thing alone, another existence, further along the same line. Is this a disappointment? Or a blessing? Or is it merely the law of all growth?"[27]

* * *

In the book we cited earlier, M. Gusdorf goes on to say that "one of the main duties of the university, in the strict sense of the term, is to act as the guarantee and the guardian of human integrity."[28] There are certain individuals who, like the ideal university, are called upon to perform this duty. By the very breadth of their research, they indicate reality's enormous complexity to those whose horizons would be narrowed by specialization and to those whose aims might be brought down too low by excessive stress on purely human considerations; they awaken their need (one which is never completely satisfied) to dominate reality with a unifying vision. Fr. Teilhard is one of these individuals. His name is written on the scroll of the heralds of "human integrity."

Does this mean he gave us a complete and perfect synthesis? Indeed it does not. Such a synthesis is unrealizable—and it would spell death to the spirit. In both intellectual and social life, the greatest objectives are those which are the most pressing, worthy of the mobilization of all energies, and the most fortunately out of reach. Moreover, the integrating of disciplines is not a totalizing of knowledge. It is the intercommunication of diverse areas of human experience, with an eye to their inner unity. And a synthesis of this kind is always a risky business. The human spirit is incapable of resting. *Quamdiu vivimus, necesse habemus semper quaerere.*[29] This is a law of the human condition and applies to the faithful and to scientists alike: *motus cogitationis in ipso remanet inquietus.*[30]

Then too, the Teilhardian synthesis is very incomplete. It belongs to a work whose major lines of development are those of a scientist, (in the strict although not in the limited sense of this term, for as Etienne Borne put it, for Teilhard "*science* is much more than just science"). This is apt to be forgotten, although Teilhard repeatedly urges his readers to bear it in mind. This work wants to be, and is, an objective "phenomenology," nothing more.[31] It stops, and nearly always with a certain tug of resolution, at the threshold of metaphysical and theological problems as such, doing little more than to point them out, formulate them, and indicate their bearings. And even when these problems are broached, even when the light of Christian revelation is focused on the question at hand, this is done— and Father Teilhard himself assures us that this is so—merely as an initial act towards a contemplation of the whole. Combining lucidity and resolution, and equipped solely with the tools of a more enlightened science, he set out to make "man's true nature" known for what it is. Those were his "tactics" as he readily admitted, and he stuck to them most of the time, leaving others the task of exploring this "true nature" in greater depth and with other methods. He made this plain to the reader. *The Phenomenon of Man,* for example, opens with the admission that, "The pages which follow do not attempt to give an explanation of the world, but only an introduction to such an explanation."[32] *Man's Place in Nature* opens in a like vein. "The pages which follow do not make the slightest claim to offer an exhaustive definition of man."[33] His most systematic essay, "La centrologie," passes over "axioms" which are felt to be "of a metaphysical nature." Its aim is to establish that an increase in "complexity" spells a like increase in "centeredness," and it restricts itself to a "law of physical recurrence" to make this point.[34] We also have his short paper of 1950 "L'Evolution de l'idée de *l'évolution*," in which he takes issue with metaphysicians who reject the theory of evolution on the grounds that it would have *"more* stemming from *less."* "Insofar as an absolute definition of man is possible in the context of the natural evolutive movement, all that the modern theory of evolution is saying is this—that in the spatio-temporal reality of the cosmos, more *follows from* less. And this is both incontestable and beyond reproach. —A *process* is not a philosophic *explanation*,"[35] As we know, two or three times he nevertheless did formulate metaphysical views, but not without specifying that there was something "risky and provisional" about them, even warning us —and stressing this very important point—that they had no necessary connection with his "dialectics" or his "apologia." In establishing his proof of personal immortality, for example, he said again and again that he was not addressing himself to "metaphysicians" but to "physicists."[36] And if we hope to make a fair-minded appraisal of Teilhard's work as a scientist who is a Christian at the same time, we would do well, whether we are considering his faith or his science, first to situate ourselves in the frame of reference which he himself chose and so carefully staked out.

Yet it is also clear that in many places a greater unity is taking shape in this work. But here again this unity is not strictly metaphysical in character. It is not so much the product of an integration painstakingly achieved through rational means; it is rather the fruit of an initial vision, ever-present in the background, continually assimilating the variety of elements which have come to light through persistent research.

Several of Fr. Teilhard de Chardin's adversaries have referred to him as a "visionary." And there is a truth hidden in this term, although it was intended to be pejorative and reflects their grossly mistaken idea about the man. Again, it was Fr. Teilhard who spoke of this "vision." He often sought strength in "a certain experience," an "inner event," which was his constant guide. This "vision" was the organizing principle in his thought, as well as its prime source of strength and unity, and the determining element in its inevitable bias.[37] This vision, this profound experience, coupled with the religious convictions of his youth and his theological thought, are responsible for the fact that his "idea" and his "basic attitude," as he called them, remained—whatever one may say to the contrary—"the same" throughout his life.[38] He often stated that this "vision was the initial, essential core, everything else developing outward from it in concentric rings, "each successive degree being less and less vital to him," —and, he added, "easier and easier to contest and to correct."[39] And finally, it is the reason why he has such an extraordinary appeal today to the most diverse casts of mind.[40]

Teilhard was, then, as Claude Cuénot has put it, "the man of vision."[41] In a general sense this can be said of everything he undertook, even of his scientific work. We recall the Foreword to The Phenomenon of Man, entitled "Seeing"; or the beginning of L'Esprit de la terre: "This is what I believe I have seen— alone and naked in front of the world."[42] And the Introduction to L'Etoffe de l'univers reminds us once again that the author is not offering us "a thesis—but an introduction; or even, if you wish, an appeal. The appeal made by a traveler who, leaving the road, finds that he has chanced onto a point of view which illuminates everything. 'Come and see!', he cries to his companions."[43] While we are using the word primarily in its religious sense, its two meanings do echo each other, for as Claude Cuénot says, Teilhard "the man of vision" is "the man of the Heart of Christ, the Heart which appears to him in glimpses and flashes throughout the universe." The letters which he wrote during the First World War, which were published a few years ago, give us some idea of the explosive force of this intense religious vision. And we are able to understand it better through *Ecrits du temps de la guerre,*[44] published at the tenth anniversary of his death, and through the correspondence in this volume. These texts are not simply the "writings of a young man" in the usual sense. (Besides, Teilhard was nearly forty when he wrote them.) In their way, they anticipate the scientific syntheses which were to blossom one after the other in the years between the wars, and they already contain the substance of *The Divine Milieu* and other apologetical or spiritual writings. Often lyrical, sometimes close to secrecy, lacking in neither dialectic rigor nor conceptual precision, they are a true reflection of the source and the initial buildings of his thought.[45]

Notes to The Aims and Scope
of the Work of Teilhard de Chardin

1. *Op. cit.,* p. 167.

2. "La maîtrise du monde et le règne de Dieu (*Ecrits,* p. 67).

3. "Ma position intellectuelle" (April, 1948), text published in *Les études philosophiques* in 1955, under the title "La pensée du Père Teilhard de Chardin par lui-même," pp. 580–581: "Critics of this philosophy have said that it is merely a generalized 'concordism.' Fr. Teilhard replied that concordism should not be confused with coherence. In the mental sphere, religion and science obviously represent two different meridians and one would err if one failed to draw a distinction between them (an error committed by concordism)." "Comment je vois" (1948), Foreword, no. 2: "It would be absurd to confuse the meridians at the equator of a sphere—this is concordism. But these same meridians must, by structural necessity, meet at the pole—this is coherence." Also see *The Phenomenon of Man,* pp. 283–285: "The Conjunction of Science and Religion"; and "Barrière de la mort et co-réflexion" (January, 1955), Appendix: "Science et revelation" (*L'Activation de l'énergie,* pp. 426–429).

4. In the Teilhardian "system" the irreversibility guaranteed by the absolute reality of Point Omega corresponds to the immortality of the soul of our classical philosophies. And while he is assured, through faith, that the "Pleroma" will one day be achieved, this assurance does not predetermine his final destiny, any more than it does that of other believers. Both the individual and the human species grow "for good . . . or ill": *Man's Place in Nature.*

136

5. In addition to the texts cited in no. 3: "La maîtrise du monde et le règne de Dieu (1916; *Ecrits*, p. 67). "Le phénomène humain" (1930) in *La vision du passé*, p. 234). "La place de l'homme dans l'univers, réflexions sur la complexité" (1942; *La vision du passé*, p. 318). *The Phenomenon of Man*, Preface, p. 30: "Like the meridians as they approach the poles, science, philosophy, and religion are bound to converge as they draw nearer to the whole. I say converge . . . but without merging, and without ceasing, to the very end, to assail the real from different angles and on different planes."

6. *Science et Christ*, p. 67; *L'Energie humaine*, p. 71. Max H. Bégouen describes in concrete terms and in a highly enjoyable style the naturally synthetic circuit of Teilhardian thought: "Ce que je dois au Père Teilhard de Chardin," in *Europe*, March–April, 1965, pp. 49–63.

7. "Comment je crois." "Mon univers," *ibid*. See "Le Christique" (1955), p. 14. See *Teilhard de Chardin, the Man and His Meaning*, pp. 39–40.

8. "Comment je vois" (1948), no. 22. But *ibid*., no. 2: Anthropogenesis and Christogenesis are "two different and partially autonomous axes."

9. *Introduction aux sciences humaines* (Paris, 1960) p. 399: "The specialist is only too willing to take his routines and his limited views for eternal truths; he protests indignantly whenever attempts are made to enlarge his field of vision, etc." See p. 144, concerning Buffon: "Today, the breadth of these immense views lies beyond our reach; our scientists have lost the cosmic generosity which is so striking in Buffon and which we will encounter again later in Lamarck. It alarmed his contemporaries in his own time; they denounced his resounding declarations because he wrote too well, and his 'systems' because he thought too 'large' . . ."

10. "Comment je vois" (1948), nos. 2 and 9.

11. "L'Hominisation" (*La vision du passé*, p. 78). Edouard Leroy often quotes from this essay (it was not published until 1957) and drew considerable material from it, as from several

other texts by Teilhard, for his *Origines humaines et l'évolution de l'intelligence* (Paris, 1928).

12. "Le phénomène humain" (1930) (*La vision du passé,* p. 234). See Maurice Corvez, *De la science à la foi, Teilhard de Chardin* (1965), pp. 126–131.

13. "L'Esprit de la terre" (1931: *L'Energie humaine,* p. 27). "The development of a new science," writes Jacques Monod, "almost always results from the fact that one science has been invaded by another, by the ideas and methods of another": "Pourquoi la France est scientifiquement sous-dévelopée" (cited in *Le Monde,* October 21, 1965, p. 9).

14. Alexandre Koyré, *Etudes d'histoire de la pensée philosophique* (Paris, 1961), pp. 231–246.

15. *The Phenomenon of Man,* p. 31 (Foreword).

16. *Op. cit.,* p. 298. See "Mon univers" (1924) (*Science et Christ,* pp. 73–74). "Esquisse d'un univers personnel" (*L'Energie humaine,* pp. 72–73).

17. "Science et Christ, ou analyse et synthèse," lecture given in Paris, February 27, 1921 (*Science et Christ,* pp. 47–62). "Mon univers" (1924); *Science et Christ,* pp. 77–81). See "La foi qui opère" (1918; *Ecrits,* p. 322). "Note sur les modes de l'action divine dans l'univers" (January, 1920). *The Phenomenon of Man,* pp. 43 and 269–272. "Esquisse d'un univers personnel" (1936; *L'Energie humaine,* p. 95). Fr. Jean Daniélou quoted Fr. Teilhard on this subject and said that he was one of those men "who go beyond the narrow compartments in which we think to contain human problems, daring to approach them in their entire breadth": *L'oraison problème politique* (Paris, 1965), p. 25.

18. "Esquisse d'un univers personnel" (*L'Energie humaine,* p. 107). François Russo, S.J., "Une double expérience spirituelle et scientifique," in *Le Monde* (April 11–12, 1965), p. 13.

19. Which does not mean, obviously, that he covered the whole subject. He never even attempted to do so.

20. "La maîtrise du monde et le règne de Dieu," Ch. 3, "L'Harmonie" (*Ecrits,* p. 80).

21. Letter of June 27, 1926.

22. *Pierre Teilhard de Chardin, Revue des questions scientifiques* (Paris, 1956), p. 101.

23. Georges Crespy has remarked with clear-sighted modesty that "There is some doubt as to whether the reformed theologian will ever be sufficiently familiar with Teilhard's theological references to fully appreciate them, and to understand the ideas and context in which they were born and have their meaning": *La pensée théologique de Teilhard de Chardin* (Paris, 1961), p. 208. Several reformed theologians have already published studies on this point; the accuracy and fair-mindedness of their work are accordingly all the more appreciated.

24. See *Teilhard de Chardin, the Man and His Meaning,* pp. 29–38, 52–55. Teilhard was already acquainted with certain of these "timid minds" who "claim that the cosmic attributes of the Pauline Christ belong only to the Divinity": "Mon univers" (1924; *Science et Christ,* p. 83).

25. Pierre Boutang, "Un chevalier de l'impossible," in *Le Monde* (April 11–12, 1965), p. 13.

26. "Ma position intellectuelle," *loc. cit.,* "Under the illuminating influence of grace, our mind recognizes Omega's manifestation (reflection) on human consciousness in the unitive properties of the Christian phenomenon; it identifies the Omega of the intellect with the Universal Christ of the Relevation." See Teilhard's second paper, December 19, 1919: ". . . the identity of God the Creator and Redeemer" (*supra,* p. 50). "Mon univers" (1924): "Christ is Omega itself" (*Science et Christ,* p. 82).

27. Letter of December 31, 1926.

28. *L'Université en question,* p. 170. This "synthesis of culture in faith and by faith" was the ideal of the old *universitas,* and our Catholic universities, despite their being in very different situations, should try to reëstablish it: Fr. Pedro Arrupe, speech delivered in Rome, October 19, 1965.

29. Hugh of St. Victor, *De sacramentis,* 1. 2, pars 14, c. 9 (*PL* 176, 570). See Pascal: "Our nature is embodied in movement; complete repose is death."

30. St. Thomas of Aquinas, *De veritate,* q. 14, art. 1, ad 5.

See H. de Lubac, *Le mystère du surnaturel* (1965), pp. 230–206.

31. See *Pensée religieuse,* pp. 244–247. The formula that we read in "Le phénomène humain" (1930) is very significant in this regard: ". . . the personality is the supreme work of nature" (*La vision du passé,* p. 242). Fr. Teilhard once pointed out one of his own weak points in the human sciences: "One of the gaps in my self-education is that I know too little about history and its sources" (*The Making of a Mind,* p. 188; March 12, 1917). He never set about to strengthen himself in this area in a methodical way.

32. *The Phenomenon of Man,* p. 29, Preface; see p. 30.

33. *Man's Place in Nature,* Preface.

34. "La centrologie, essai d'une dialectique de l'union" (Peking, December 13, 1944), no. 26 (*L'Activation de l'énergie,* p. 120). Earlier, "La vie cosmique" (*Ecrits,* p. 9); "Mon univers" (1924; *Science et Christ,* p. 74).

35. *Bulletin de l'Union catholique des scientifiques français,* discussion of religious thought faced with evolution (*La vision du passé,* pp. 347–348).

36. *The Singularities of the Human Species* (1935). See "Esquisse d'un univers personnel": "All that we offer to the positivist knowledge of our century is a principle of succession in duration; a law of recurrence. —Not a metaphysics, let us repeat, but an ultraphysics" (*L'Energie humaine,* p. 111). "Comment je vois" (1948), no. 25, etc. "We feel that he is uncomfortable in the first philosophy," wrote Georges Crespy, *op. cit.,* p. 114, and Teilhard himself, we think, would not deny this.

37. See *Teilhard de Chardin, the Man and His Meaning,* the Preface in particular. See Christian d'Armagnac, S.J., "Le premier Teilhard: le Christ et le monde," in *Etudes* (May, 1965), p. 653: "Teilhard first evolved a Christocentric spirituality and vision of the universe and life . . . A religious and spiritual research was the dominant element in the first ten years of Teilhard's literary activity, from 1916 to 1926, from "La vie cosmique" to *The Divine Milieu.* And as he meditated

on the war, it was this research which stimulated and awakened him and which made him a writer."

38. These terms are found in a letter to G. B. Barbour, dated Paris, April 15, 1949. George B. Barbour, *In the Field with Teilhard de Chardin* (New York, 1965), pp. 125–127. Teilhard's thought, in its totality, "harbors the nugget of pure gold which has the piety and faith of his youth—it lies intact, as if it has been miraculously preserved beneath continual deposits of scientific or philosophic material. He himself stressed this continuity, an element essential to the understanding of his writings." Etienne Gilson, "Le cas Teilhard de Chardin," in *Seminarium,* 17, 1965, p. 727.

39. "Mon univers" (1918), Preface (*Ecrits,* p. 267). See "Le Christique" (1955).

40. We cite one of the many testimonies to this widespread appeal, by Gaston Roupnel, published earlier in *Cahiers Pierre Teilhard de Chardin,* vol. 4 (1963), pp. 132–133. Roupnel wrote us on January 17, 1946, that "The manuscripts of Fr. Teilhard de Chardin opened my eyes to new truths, brought illumination to my pained and flagging soul, breathed life into my suffocating spiritual forces . . . It seemed to me that in reading them, everything that had been disjointed and rough in my thinking took on form and unity, and my mind was thrilled. . . . The highest aims and strictest logic of science took on meaning and life in this Christian credo. The Incarnation, the Redemption, the Resurrection, the Communion gathered in and contained the whole world. . . ."

41. *Pierre Teilhard de Chardin,* Paris, 1958, p. 473.

42. The words *and naked* do not appear in the manuscript from which the printed text was taken, *L'Energie humaine,* p. 25.

43. *L'Activation de l'énergie,* p. 398. "Within sight of St. Helena Island (the crossing from New York to Capetown), July 14, 1953."

44. Pierre Teilhard de Chardin, *Ecrits du temps de la guerre, 1916–1919* (Paris, 1965); essays, with a Commentary by Mgr. Bruno de Solages and Fr. Henri de Lubac. See letter to Léon-

tine Zanta, August 7, 1923: "It was the flowering of ideas during the war . . ."

45. One can read of Fr. Teilhard's concern for synthesis in the volume in tribute to Fr. Bochenski (Fribourg, 1965), Chapter XVI by Fr. Norbert M. Luyten, O.P.: "Réflexions sur la méthode de Teilhard de Chardin" (pp. 290–314).

"Ascent" and "Descent" in the Work of Teilhard de Chardin

There is a key, we are told, "opening all locks; within it a Christian works in vain, however capable and learned he may be. Whatever the question we are facing, whether it be the manifestation of the world, or of life, or of the human soul, the appearance of sanctifying grace, or of Christ, our *first* consideration must be the *movement of descent* by which the divinity, breaking with what preceded, inaugurates a new, superior, and discontinuous order; *only then,* through the *movement of ascent,* does a preëxisting being proceed continuously towards its appropriate ends, or prepare, under the influence of an elevating motion, an order beyond its reach."

This view is so fundamental and, taken as a whole, so true, that every believer would do well to accept it. We will attempt one note of clarification here, hoping not to weaken its force but only to anticipate a possible misunderstanding in its application. When we are told that the "movement of descent"—that is, divine initiative in the many forms it takes—must be "considered first," and that "only then" may the "movement of ascent" —that is, the progress of a being, its passing through one order to a superior one—be considered, it is clear that this "first" and "only then" refer to a thing's progress in the real, ontological sequence, and not necessarily to the order in which it is invented, discovered, or in which findings about it are published. By quoting these lines we do not mean to imply that a scientist must, for example, declare his view on divine causality before publishing his experimental observations on the limits of brute matter and of life. Let us suppose that for our human intelligence, the normal order is to begin in the created universe and to climb to God. Normally, then, the scientist must first consider the progress (if there is any) realized in the bosom of nature—for example, the ascent of matter to life, then of vegetable or animal life to the human—in order then to be able to look for and explain the source of this increase of being. When a biologist or paleontologist observes (accurately or inaccurately, it does not matter here) an ascensional movement in the procedure of the universe, and is content to describe this process experimentally, going no further than that, no one will reproach him his description as disrespectful to the Divinity. Then if he goes further, acting not only as a scientist but as a philosopher, his goal being to locate the source of the progress observed in a divine causality, here too no one will reproach him for not having pursued this goal from the very beginning! He does not deny this causality in not speaking of it. In mentioning it second, he does not claim it is not first in its effects; in other words, he does not maintain that the "movement of descent" (to stay with this term) does not precede the "movement of ascent." Although it was discovered second, and discussed second, the "movement of descent" is nevertheless affirmed as the first of the two movements.

Perhaps we should excuse ourselves for making such an obvious statement. But it has its purpose, as will be seen in a moment.

Let us bear it in mind as we look at the work of Fr. Teilhard de Chardin. In *The Phenomenon of Man* Fr. Teilhard analyzes the ascensional motion of the universe up to and through man. In his religious essays he describes the ascension of the soul and the growth of the Mystical Body, up to the attainment of divine union. He outlines a "Christogenesis." If in both of these cases he does not recognize God's absolute priority as he should, it is because there should be no need to do so. However, he has been attacked thus: "The evolutive vision aims at taking a doctrine which is not of this world and transposing its truths into a perspective of ascent. No, this the Church will never allow."

This simple sentence—itself irreproachable in the statement it makes—seems to us to be clouded with confusion. True, Fr. Teilhard spoke several times of a "transposition." This is a word from his vocabulary. But he never spoke of bringing about the kind of transformation which seems to be attributed to him here. The only form of "transposition" with any apparent connection to the one cited above is his transposition of the idea of "cosmos" into the idea of "cosmogenesis." Plainly, this is quite another matter. In a letter of January 1, 1951, for example, he urges that "the vision which is traditionally explained in terms of a Cosmos be transposed into the dimensions of a Cosmogenesis." In other words, according to him, a static vision should be replaced by a dynamic one; what this means, then, is that if Christ actually does have an influence on and a mastery over the cosmos, as St. Paul maintains, the idea of a "Christ evolutor" is a rather fitting way of conceiving of this influence and mastery.[1] A "transposition" of this kind, and the transfer involved, raises more than one major problem, as Fr. Teilhard himself fully realizes.[2] However pertinent one may judge these problems to be, there is nothing in all of this which would substitute an ascending perspective for a descending one (that is, if the latter term is not taken to be a "regressive evolution" of our universe, clearly irrelevant to our subject). No doubts whatever are raised concerning the descending perspective belonging to our Christian faith. In fact, whenever Teilhard speaks of the descending perspective—in other words, of the priority of God, of divine action, of divine initiative—he indicates it clearly enough.

* * *

First of all, let us note that this very term *descent,* in the sense in which it was used in our opening passage, is encountered fairly frequently in his work—and with the very same meaning; "The Fire which Descends" is one of the subtitles of *Le Milieu mystique.*[3] *The Mass of the World* (1923) cele-

brates "the ray descending from the Heart of God."[4] In 1936
his "Esquisse d'un univers personnel" established "the presence,
today, of a terminal divine Center" and adds this essential detail, that "In Him everything rises as towards a center of immanence. But from Him everything also descends as from a
summit of transcendence."[5] In 1939 an article on "La mystique
de la science," published in *Etudes,* explained the same idea
by the same word, this time not only in connection with God,
but in regard to the Incarnation. "An ascending anthropogenesis
is an ideal background and base for the descending illumina-
tions of a Christogenesis."[6] Again, in a brief essay of 1950,
"How May We Conceive and Hope that Human Unanimisation
will be Realized on Earth?", we read that "A world culminating
in the Impersonal can bring us neither the warmth of attraction
nor the hope of irreversibility (immortality) without which individual egotism will always have the last word. . . . It seems that
Man's urge towards *Some Thing* ahead of him cannot achieve
its full fruition except by combining with another and still more
fundamental aspiration—one from above, urging him towards
Some One."[7] We find the verb *to fall* used in a similar sense in
The Divine Milieu. "The deviations of the pantheists testify to our
immense need for a word of revelation falling from the lips of
Him who is." In the same work, as well as in "Mon univers"
(1924) and a lecture entitled "Science and Christ," the author
quotes (summarizing somewhat) from the Epistle to the Ephesians: "*Quod autem ascendit, quid est, nisi quod prius descendit,
ut repleret omnia?*"[8] "First and foremost, the movement of descent"—how could he have put it better?

But the vocabulary is not everything. Without even employ-
ing the word *descent* a number of other Teilhardian texts
assure us that their author had a firm grip on "the key opening
all locks." Obviously, he had little occasion to use it in his
scientific writings, although we do see it there at his elbow,
ready to be of service. Here, for example, is how *The Phenomenon of Man,* a work which restricts itself to objective
phenomenology, describes the decisive step from animal to man:
"It [the animal] is separated from us by a chasm—or a

146

threshold—impassable for it. Because we are reflective, we are not only different from the animal, we are another kind of being altogether. This isn't just one form of progress among many; it is 'a mutation from zero to all.' Not simply a change in degree, —but a change in nature, —resulting from a change in condition."[9] We note the word *impassable*. Elsewhere this separation is spoken of as "major discontinuity," or as "discontinuity of the first order," as "ontological discontinuity"; it is also expressed as a "rupture between man and all that preceded him, this being the basic fact, presented as scientifically as possible,"[10] which too many scientists ignore or reject. Does he see this step from animality to the human kingdom merely as a "movement of ascent"? Does he profess the idea of an ascending "continuity" which operates on its own initiative, without intervention of any superior causality, without any new principle? "The rising tide of consciousness we share in is not merely the product of an exertion we summon from ourselves . . . A heavenly body raises it."[11]

Fr. Teilhard often pursued phenomenological analysis to the point of "the inevitable intrusion . . . of the problem of God."[12] He then showed the world to be "entirely suspended from above, to Omega."[13] Thus he says, for example, in *L'Esprit de la terre* (1913), that "[we witness] the reappearance of the traditional concepts of a God intellectually influencing immortal monads, distinct from Himself."[14] Could this intellectual influence, or divine revelation, be anything else but a major instance of the "movement of descent" quoted at the beginning of our essay? He refers to it again towards the end of *The Future of Man* (1941), a work where one would little expect to encounter it: "The generative principle of its [the earth's] unification is finally to be sought, not in the contemplation of a single Truth or in the sole desire for a single Thing, but in the common attraction exercised by a single Being."[15] The attraction exercised by this "single Being," that is, by the Living God, is thus a drawing force towards the "principle"—the "first" of all—although it is not revealed here until the end. It is certainly first in regard to all evolution, to all ascent achieved by man.

147

"Omega, in which everything converges, is in turn the source of everything radiated."[16]

It is natural to Fr. Teilhard to gear his research to "the order in which things were invented," and he invites us to carry this practice on after him. He proceeds, therefore, *per ascensum*. He uses this method in the construction of his "hyperphysics," as opposed to a "metaphysics" which would proceed *per descensum,* or which would unfold "primarily in the realm of essences, and then, by that fact alone, in the realm of possibility itself."[17] Putting it more simply, we might say that his method is inductive, not deductive.[18] Need we point out that nothing is more warranted and more indicated? This does not mean he wants to locate Being at the culminating point of a cosmic ascent. On the contrary, "the elementary cosmic centers" which we ourselves are, "secure immortality" through being received by Being—by the transcendent and preëxisting Omega.[19] We find further support for this in the essay "Super-Humanité, Super-Christ, Super-Charité" (1943). Having carried "the lines of the human phenomenon to their natural limit," the author follows his usual method and suggests an about-face. "Here we might switch our viewpoint end for end. In other words, having tried to advance from bottom to top, following in the experimental footsteps of science, we might look at things from top to bottom, starting from the summits where we place Christianity and religion."[20]

An essay dating from 1946, "L'Esquisse d'une dialectique de l'esprit," is even more specific. In this work Fr. Teilhard sets out to clarify the steps of his dialectic. It proceeds, he informs us, through four stages. Beginning with the scientific observation, they form the four phases of what he calls (here and in other places) his "apologia."

The first stage is set forth in a limited number of essays and takes him from the "phenomenon of man" (which for him sums up all earlier phenomenon) to "the transcendent, ingathering, irreversible Omega." Thus the "evolutive creation" has been established, and the second stage leads on to "God, the motive force and revealer." During the third stage, we pass from the "Christian phenomenon," still observed from the outside, to the recognition of "God incarnate." Finally, the fourth stage leads from "the living Church" to "Christ-Omega." Our purpose here is not to analyze, verify, or discuss the details of this dialectic, but, as we have attempted previously, to try to reach an impartial decision as to whether Fr. Teilhard does or does not "transpose" the truths of Christian faith (that is, "of a doctrine which is not of this world") in such a way as to betray them in the "perspective of ascent" of his "evolutive vision."

We see that there is nothing of the sort in stage one. Whether we approach it from above or below, we find that there can only be a pure ascending movement between the "phenomenon of man" and "Omega," as in reality itself. "Seen from below, from our vantage point, the apex of the evolutive cone (the point Omega) stands out on the horizon as a center of convergence, purely immanent—humanity engrossed in contemplating itself. But on closer study we realize that this center, in order to hold together, must have behind it, yet more profound than it, a transcendent nucleus—necessarily divine." This indeed reassures us. Yet the divine action is not wholly clear by the end of the first stage. As we noted earlier, several of Fr. Teilhard's works set out to take us to this point, but no further. They do not claim to treat of all the problems of theism or, a fortiori, of the Christian revelation, for these subjects must be handled by other means of research.[21] In the Outline to his dialectic Fr. Teilhard says, "The reason why some people are taken aback by a number of my essays is largely due to the fact that, writing for non-believers, I do not go beyond Phase One in my reasoning." But now we move on to the second stage, where the "humano-cosmic phenomenon" comes forward in a new light, "profoundly modified." At first, all that was to be seen here (or that we could make out) was an autonomous, spontaneous movement of rising consciousness. But now we discover that this flux is a tide rising through the action of a supreme heavenly body. God is an "attracting" force, and the elements of the world are "attracted." The ascensional movement of the world is compared to the flux of the tide. Thus, the priority of divine attraction is established. With this, the supreme nature of this divine attraction on man is announced, defined, and localized—as the Revelation.[22]

Once we have recognized the fact of this "revelation coming from above" (here again, the "movement of descent"), this revelation which culminates in the Incarnation, "a spark flying back and forth *through a personal milieu* between God and the Universe, to reascend a third time to the apex of being, then we no longer perceive it merely as a center of consciousness, nor as a first psychic motive alone, nor even as a being which speaks, but as the Word which incarnates itself. The universe does not raise itself progressively towards unity merely by virtue of an external force acting on it; it does so because the Transcendent has made Itself partially immanent here. This is the message of the Revelation." Thus the "movement of descent" is not only discernible as a first causality, a motive force, influence, attraction, and illumination. It is—to the extent that this word can be applied to the Divinity—the actual descent of God to man, His "humiliation" in the incarnation of the Word, as the Fathers say according to the Scriptures; and as a popular hymn has it, His "abasement." "Kenosis, supreme humility, excentration, *movement of descent*," writes Fr. Teilhard in one of his contemplative pieces. These are his own terms. The "movement of descent" is initiated first. Our "movement of ascent" (which can happen "only then") is totally dependent on it.

This personal movement of ascent, dependent on the Incarnation, begins by faith, "theological faith"; and again it is clear that God makes His descent to us first, for the act of faith presupposes the initiative of the Word *fides ex auditu*[23] and can only be produced "under the influence of grace." This is how we are gathered into the "living Church," to be led at last to the transcendent Trinitarian center," always "under the mediating action of Christ-Omega."[24]

The more spiritual of Fr. Teilhard's writings make even clearer, if possible, the absolute priority of the divine action in all stages of the work of salvation. In *The Divine Milieu* Fr.

Teilhard quotes St. Paul, who told the Areopagites of "God, who made man that he might seek Him," —and then goes on to say that, "In accordance with His promise, God truly waits for us in things, unless indeed He steps forward to meet us." The believer cannot doubt this divine initiative which awaits him in everything, always: "Yes, O my God, I believe it . . . It is you who are at the origin of the impulse, you who are at the heart of the attraction which I pursue single-mindedly throughout my life, and whose initial pulses and development I favor. . . . It is you yourself whom I find, you who make me participate in your being . . . I shall collaborate in your prevenient action . . . O God, whose call precedes the very first of our movements, grant me the desire to desire being—that, by means of the divine thirst which is your gift, the access to the great waters may open wide within me."[25]

The believer not only recognizes God as "the original source" of his natural being, of his moral acts, and of his "divine thirst"; he also knows that God has undertaken—historically, if this can be said—the work of "intimately uniting Himself" with His created. Such is the mystery of Jesus. Now "the power of the Word incarnate streams into Matter," and for the Christian who lives his faith "the boundless magic of the divine milieu owes, finally, all its concrete value to the divino-human contact revealed in the Epiphany of Jesus." Jesus Christ, Jesus of Nazereth, son of the Virgin, is "the radiant sun of love come to illuminate the world" and to communicate the might of His Spirit to us. Here is another series of expressions which draw us towards this same truth. Their message is unmistakable; they are urging us towards the realization that everything comes to us "first" through the divinity's "movement of descent," inaugurating "a new superior order."

"*Posuit homines . . . si forte attrectent eum.* His prevenient grace is therefore always on the alert to excite our first look and our first prayer. But in the end the initiative, the awakening, always come from Him, and whatever the further developments of our mystical faculties, no progress is achieved in this domain except as the new response to a new gift. *Nemo venit ad me,*

151

nisi Pater traxerit eum . . . Lord, . . . send us your spirit, *Spiritus principalis,* whose flaming action alone can effect the birth and achievement of the great metamorphosis which sums up all the inward perfection and towards which your creation yearns: *Emitte Spiritum tuum, et creabuntur, et renovabis faciem terrae.*" Much later, during one of his retreats, he wrote, "Completely suspended to Him: in my cohesion, my action, even in my perception of, and passion for, Him."[26]

Thus, all the initiative lies with God. God comes to man, and during salvation, is responsible for everything that happens within man. All He asks is our fidelity. "Through fidelity and fidelity alone can we return to God the kiss He is forever offering us across the world." Man may sometimes delude himself but soon "he is grasped by what he thought he had seized."[27] And then he understands, as Fr. Teilhard wrote on the feast of the Presentation, that "the attitude that incorporates us fully with the truth is indeed that of the Presentation, in which we humbly expose ourselves to the radiation of the infinite Being, ardently longing that He may penetrate us and transform us into Himself."[28]

Thus, according to Fr. Teilhard, fidelity, combined with faith and purity, is the great force animating "the individual advances of the divine milieu." It is one of the three virtues, which are "immobile in appearance but which are, in reality, active among things," and make up man's response to the prevenient activity of Him who said of Himself, "Ego operor," and who said of His Father, "Pater semper operatur."[29] Even if we had none of the texts cited earlier, this reference alone would be enough to convince us that Fr. Teilhard had the key well in hand, the key "opening all locks"—the key that every Christian should take up—and that in meditating on his universe, he did not work "in vain."

Fr. Teilhard de Chardin wrote *The Divine Milieu* at Tientsin, in the winter of 1926–1927. As we know, he wrote a similar tract earlier, "Le milieu mystique," dating from the summer of 1917. This work is more revealing of his personal experience. In it he speaks of the transformation which God desires to bring

152

about within us, "in the course of which, all that man can do is to cultivate an inner openness and to humbly accept." We quote from the final page. Here the ways of divine initiative are elaborated and refined, so to speak, so as to cut short any tendency to limit the scale and gratuitousness of the "movement of descent." "God appears as the only being capable of sustaining and guiding mystical thought, from its first humble awakening onward. Even though we can artificially induce certain transitory tremors of excitement, the taste for life—the source of all passion and vision, even divine—does not really belong to us. We are unable to modify that place deep within ourselves where the light of life burns. All we do is to receive ourselves. It is God who instils the desire in us to want Him. And if the soul is eager for heaven, it is still unable to perceive the object of its desire unless it is helped to do so. The soul can only see God if God looks at it. This is true too on the human plane, one man being unable to force another to turn towards him and see him! Thus at last, when the soul has discerned the fiery Center which has sought it, it is powerless to climb up the ray playing upon it and to throw itself into the light. . . . For it is written, 'No one comes unto me if I do not take him up and attract him myself unto myself.' Mystical beatitude culminates in the consciousness of this gratuitousness, this supreme dependence. —*Qui potest capere, capiat.*"[30]

In 1921 in Paris, Fr. Teilhard told a group of young Christians, "Through existence itself we have become the conscious co-workers in a creation which continues through us, in all likelihood to take us to a goal (even a terrestrial one) much more elevated and distant than anything we can imagine. We should aid God with all our strength, and manipulate matter as though our salvation depended on our industry alone." Here he was paraphrasing St. Paul's *Dei adjutores sumus* and extolling human effort. But he quickly added that a Christian should have a clear understanding of the spirit in which one should take this effort up. "If one thinks about it, the attempt to force the doors of the ultralife amorally or immorally, as did the Titans, is impossible and contradictory. . . . Should we do as the Titans?

—Impossible. . . . The further we advance . . . the more we should adore."[31] Three years later, alluding to those who seemed to "conceive of the search for a religion as a vast scientific enterprise," he wrote, "It is only too clear that the Absolute is not disposed to being 'taken by force' but must 'give itself' (manifest itself) to the minds which await it."[32] And in a second version of his "Univers," adopting Blondel's principle that "everything holds together from above" (as he had done previously in 1918 in his "Foi qui opère" and again in *The Phenomenon of Man*), he developed its principal philosophic implications in the realm of cosmology. Then, undertaking the theological part of his exposition, and alluding to the movement of descent which stems from the Word of God and which precedes and founds the ascendant elaboration of the Pleroma, he said, "When Christ appeared in the arms of Mary, He had just raised the World." After reading this sentence, who could still believe that Fr. Teilhard thought the world lifts itself on its own force? In writing about the work of redemption of the World incarnate, he said, "Let us try to gather the mass of passions, expectations, fears, troubles, and happiness into one Ocean, each man representing a drop. This is the immense sea that Christ plunged into until He completely absorbed it, through every pore. This is the tumultuous sea which He diverted in His powerful heart, until He had subdued its waves and tides to the rhythm of His life." This is the meaning of the passionate life of the beneficent, praying Christ. And this too is the incomparable virtue of His death on the cross."[33]

For the last time, then, does this amount to "taking a doctrine which is not of this world and transposing its truths into a perspective of ascent?"

* * *

We are led to ask how such a misunderstanding could have arisen. Again, it seems to us, from a "transposition." But this time the transposition is not the doing, real or imagined, of Fr.

Teilhard, but of several of his critics. Clearly, they overlooked many passages in his work, or read them inattentively. But more than that, they took material which he treated as science and phenomenology and transposed it into metaphysics, theology, or spirituality, a quite unwarranted maneuver.

This idea of an ascensional dynamism is central to Fr. Teilhard's thought. For him, the cosmos is a "cosmogenesis." Evolution is universal and proceeds towards an objective; in its "fundamental thrust" it realizes a progress in being, a growth of psychism, an increase in unity. All his scientific work tends to support the concept that the "phenomenon of man" becomes *the* great phenomenon. Man "transcends all categories of Linnean systematics, and all earlier formulas of biological evolution." He appears as the "uppermost shoot of the tree of life," the "direction-post of the world of growth," the "arrow flying towards the center of an ingathering universe"; he is the "principal axis of growth," the "frontal wave of a universe which glows as it folds inward upon itself."[34] "[He presents] the history of the universe," comments Fr. N. M. Wildiers, "not as a disorderly unfolding, as a succession of highs and lows, or as a pitch and well between two poles, but quite to the contrary as a gradual ascension in a well-determined and irreversible direction. . . ."[35]

All Teilhardian phenomenology as presented in the two principal works *The Phenomenon of Man* (directly derived from a whole series of papers) and *Man's Place in Nature* tends to lay the groundwork for this concept. "Humanity constitutes a front of cosmic advance." Like "vitalization," hominisation is the conquest over an "ontological discontinuity."[36] Here Fr. Teilhard was taking issue with the concepts current, even dominant, in his day, in science and in other areas—concepts which are still fairly prevalent today. He explained this on a number of occasions. For example, we read in *Man's Place in Nature,* "Life is an epiphenomenon of matter, —just as thought is an epiphenomenon of life; isn't this what altogether too many people think, at least implicitly?" In the logic of present-day systematics, "the human group represents nothing but a miser-

155

able marginal subdivision ('family') in the tableau of the vertebrates . . ." We are blind to the fact that this group "acts functionally as the unique and terminal 'inflorescence' of the tree of life."[37]

Fr. Teilhard tried to demonstrate "the dazzling grandeur of the human achievement," its "majesty" and "incomparable pathos."[38] In doing so he opposed the "false modesty" of a number of scientific men who represent a hold-over from the thought of the last century. He took them to account for their "anatomical prejudices." "Left to itself, pure zoology is quite unable to provide us with a clue which might lead us out of the labyrinth of living forms weaving the biosphere."[39] He hoped to show that the advent of man is "the greatest telluric and biological event of our planet." In the face of their phobia of anthropocentrism, he set out to establish that "Man, the center of perspective, is at the same time the *center of construction* of the universe."[40] "Is it our fault," he asked, "if we coincide with the axis of things?" He opposed all those who fail to recognize the value of man, whether through myopia—"the feeble morphological variation which gave rise to reflective thought" blinding them to "the enormous shock which the appearance of this new faculty produced in the general distribution of terrestrial life"—or whether through an obstinate commitment to some doctrine such as materialism, agnosticism, or some other form of *a priori* reasoning. For "four centuries," he maintained, these minds have persisted in dissolving man "in the average of things," in characterizing consciousness as "an anomaly," "a fortuitous accident, bizarre, aberrant, accidental in the universe."[41] They have continued to speak of "man's insignificance in the presence of the rest of nature," or at least have caused his most precious spiritual activities to come to nothing, to disappear like a spark swallowed up in the night. As Fr. Teilhard took his stand against them, he set out to prove that man "isn't simply a new 'species' of animal (as is still said only too often today); he represents and announces *a new species of life*."[42] In September, 1928, at the conclusion of the first of his papers (unpublished until

1965) entitled *The Phenomenon of Man,* he had already proclaimed his hope and his position. "Humanity, considered for a long time a scientific accessory or an aberrant element of the universe, will end up discovering itself the fundamental phenomenon—*the* phenomenon par excellence of nature . . ."[43] And in 1955, in "Les singularités de l'espèce humaine," he took up the cause a last time, hoping that man, "who by dint of his extreme organic arrangement and extreme psychic interiorisation, should by rights form the structural key of the universe," might no longer be "treated as an accident or an incident in nature."[44]

This is the heart of his "message." It has been restated recently by one of his co-workers, Fr. Pierre Leroy. "Those who were able to understand its content and value found it extremely heartening. No longer is man 'this miserable mould,' this poor fool, this animal, intelligent certainly but nevertheless destined, like his fellow animals, to spend several years on an inhospitable and cruel earth, and then to disappear without a trace . . . The universe refound its greatness, man his transcendence, the entire human group its brilliant function as the world's, and creation's, worker. We revived to a hope dimmed by unprecedented catastrophies, by rash acts committed by a technology ready to try anything. Man took on meaning; the earth took on meaning. To our contemporaries, betrayed and deprived of the true light by both materialistic and existential philosophies, Fr. Teilhard's message was a long-awaited cure."[45]

Fr. Teilhard found himself at odds with still another group of intellectuals, due to his views on cosmogenesis and the phenomenon of man. Although the tone here is rather informal, allow us to go back a little and quote from a letter he wrote us from Tien-tsin on July 31, 1930; it testifies, by the way, to his good sense in being able to resist the scientific "fashions" of the day.[46] "*La Revue des questions scientifiques* has asked me to send them an article entitled 'Notes on "the phenomenon of man."' [47] In writing it, I managed to put down quite a few things that are dear to me—and a certain number of them won't exactly class me up with the 'advanced' of science. My theme is that man is the key to understanding the universe (the uni-

157

verse becoming, for every true science, basically an *irreversible* progression of the spirit). Now then, we find that there are quite a few physicists (or talkers) who are standing behind Einstein, their prophet, and beginning to proclaim the existence of a finite and reversible universe where space, the only definite and fundamental reality, is supposed to make duration disappear. All this strikes me as a delirium of geometrisation in ultra-specialized minds. These ideas would destroy all faith, all morals, even all taste for research. But that doesn't make them any less prevalent. And with this, I'm finding myself classed among the outdated."[48]

When Pascal celebrated the dignity of rational man, he did not pit man against God; he exalted his dignity with respect to a material universe, this blind, deaf universe which crushes man "without even realizing it is doing so." Likewise, when Teilhard pictures man at the forefront of the ascensional movement of nature, dominating nature through "his infinite complexity," he does not do so to contrast him with a creature dependent on the Creator! When he says that "man can serve man to decipher the world," he is simply urging us to recognize that "nature resists our efforts to understand her" as long as we "go about her the wrong way, against the grain," in other words by "the material and the plural," instead of heeding the evidence of the "conscious" and the "free."[49] There are certain people who cannot be expected to appreciate Teilhard's accomplishment: those who are unaware of the problems raised in our time by the natural sciences, or of the obnubilations caused in a great number by their development; minds which, in dealing in science and methodology, are satisfied with mediocre standards; certain theologians who are entrenched in their specialties. Clearly, such people are incapable of recognizing the greatness or pertinence of Teilhard's work. At the very least one could ask them to recall, for example, Gabriel Séailles' "Pourquoi les dogmes ne renaissent pas," from his *Les affirmations de la conscience moderne,* a work which enjoyed such a great success during the first thirty years of our century;[50] and then, in this context, to reread the Teilhardian formulas concerning cosmogenesis and anthropogenesis. Having done this, if they still do not have a clear picture of the positive value of these formulas, we hope that they will at least understand that they do not contain an attitude disrespectful to the Divinity.[51] For they do not compromise divine causality in general, or any of the gratuitous initiatives such as the Revelation, the Incarnation, or grace. None of them is in the least contradictory to the primacy of the "movement of descent"! It is pointless to try to link them with Prometheus, the Titans, Babel, Faust, or Nietzsche. Those who think they are defeating Teilhard really share his views wholeheartedly, for it is he who sets out to "eliminate attitudes of harshness and pride from the scientific conquest of the world." We have already seen him repudiate any undertaking smacking of the "impossible" and "immoral" enterprise of the Titans. On several different occasions he brings up the Promethean myth,[52] using it to clarify the teachings of the Christian faith by virtue of its sharp dissimilarity to them. He calls it "the age-old pride," and "the temptation of heroism which has existed throughout the ages." He proposes two forms of "battle" against God so that he might set them off one from the other, that of Prometheus or Satan on the one hand, an out-and-out revolt, and that of Jacob on the other, the very soul of adoration.[53]

In casting man as the "key to evolution" and, consequently, as "the key to understanding the universe," in showing us that in the vision he urges us to share with him, "man becomes ever more meaningful,"[54] Teilhard de Chardin does not diminish the glory of God. In the last essay he wrote, he says that this "supreme glory" is the ultimate criterion.[55] The only divinity he diminishes in stature is the pseudo-divinity, universal entrophy, —"the majestic and inflexible entrophy," the "disheartening entrophy," "this great leveler of cosmic energy."[56] A certain branch of learning has considered it "*the* one and only primeval, definitive current" and has seen to immerse man in it completely. We seemed doomed to lie buried under this "rain of ashes" forever. But in establishing the victory of the "imponderable current of the mind" over the "ponderable current of entrophy," of the "conscious ordered" over the "unconscious unordered," of the complex and improbable over the homogenous and probable, or as he said, of evolution over involution,[57] he has brought about the resurgence of "the human paradox."[58] Thus he established the conditions which would permit "God's face" to shine forth again "in our present-day universe," "more radiant than ever before."[59] Now "the fact of man" is restored "to its proper place"; and "as man takes on fresh importance in nature," the idea of a personal God can be reborn; in fact, this renaissance is already making itself felt. Henceforth, the road is clear so that "the spirit of the earth, with the high degree of self-mastery it has recently attained, can now become conscious of its increasingly vital need to adore. God emerges from universal evolution to impress Himself upon your consciousness, greater and more necessary than ever before."[60] Religion can no longer be considered "a primitive, transitory stage which humanity goes through during infancy." The religious function is born of hominisation and is tied to it, and cannot help but grow with man himself.[61] The more human man becomes, the more necessary will it be for him to know how to adore and to be able to do so. By the same token, the clearer will be his understanding—one hopes, at least—"that Christian mystical theology should become the basic, universal mystical theology of tomorrow."[62] Since the time of Pascal, new and much more earnest attempts have been made to deprive man of his "supereminent dignity." In restoring this dignity to man, and doing this through new means, Fr. Teilhard de Chardin makes "fidelity" and "adoration" possible once again. He restores "the joy of adoration" to man.[63]

Notes to "Ascent" and "Descent" in the Work of Teilhard de Chardin

1. See Christopher F. Mooney, S.J., "The Body of Christ in the Writings of Teilhard de Chardin," in *Theological Studies*, 25 (1964), p. 579: "Frequently in his theological writings he [Teilhard] repeats that what he is doing is simply transposing into an evolutionary framework the great cosmic affirmations of St. Paul regarding the Person of Christ." And *ibid.*, pp. 594–596.

2. "Comment je vois," Appendix 2: "Note au phénomène chrétien." See Mooney, "Teilhard de Chardin and the Christological Problem," in *The Harvard Theological Review*, 58 (1965), pp. 91–126. However, the "transposition of concepts" which Teilhard considered necessary and which he felt must be "deep" should, according to him, "save the value of the world without touching God": "Action et activation" (1945; *Science et Christ*, p. 228).

3. *Ecrits du temps de la guerre*, p. 161.

4. Edition de 1965 (Ed. du Seuil), p. 56.

5. *L'Energie humaine*, pp. 87–88.

6. *L'Energie humaine*, p. 221.

7. *The Future of Man*, pp. 287–288.

8. *The Divine Milieu*, p. 30. "Panthéisme et christianisme" (1923). "Science et Christ" (1921; *Science et Christ*, p. 62). "Mon univers" (1924; *Science et Christ*, p. 92). And in "La parole attendue" (1940; *Cahiers Pierre Teilhard de Chardin*, vol. 4, p. 27). Eph. 4, 9–10. Fr. Pierre Leroy recalls having "asked Fr. Teiland one day what text in the Scriptures would best sum up his philosopy and mysticism. He quoted me this

sentence from St. Paul: *Descendit, ascendit, ut impleret omnia;* Christ descended, then ascended, that He might fill all things" (J.A.F., June 1958).

9. Pp. 149 and 171. See Teilhard's second paper for Maurice Blondel: ". . . the spiritual soul's invasion of the body . . ." (*supra*, p. 44).

10. "Le phénomène humain" (1930; *La vision du passé*, pp. 233–234). "La place de l'homme dans la nature" (1932; *La vision du passé*, p. 253).

11. "Comment je vous" (1948), no. 24. "L'Esprit de la terre" (1931): ". . . By following along the path of simple immanence, we have traced the cosmic phenomenon *of the within*. But by the very logic of this path, we find ourselves forced . . . to recognize that the current which raises matter should be thought of as a tide, rather than a simple internal thrust" (*L'Energie humaine,* p. 56). "L'Hominisation" (1925; *La vision du passé,* p. 104; see pp. 323–324). In the course of biological evolution, whenever there is an addition and increase in being, we must suppose a creative contribution, and "in the case of man, whose soul is becoming spiritual, one should realize that this contribution is enormous." Letter to Louis Richard, October 20, 1924.

12. "A Biological Interpretation of Human History" 1947; *The Future of Man,* p. 181). See "Sauvons l'humanité" (1936; *Science et Christ,* p. 187). "Some Reflections on the Spiritual Repercussions of the Atom Bomb," closing words: ". . . the problem of God" (1946; *The Future of Man,* p. 148). *Man's Place in Nature,* August 4, 1949: ". . . And if I am not mistaken, it is at this point that the problem of God . . . presents itself in the science of evolution . . ." "La convergence de l'univers," final note (1951; *L'Activation de l'énergie,* p. 309).

13. "La centrologie," no. 32 (1944; *L'Activation de l'énergie,* p. 133).

14. "L'Esprit de la terre" (*L'Energie humaine,* p. 56).

15. *The Future of Man,* p. 75. See "La vie cosmique": "There is something absolute which both attracts us and remains concealed . . ." (1916; *Ecrits,* p. 18). *The Phenomenon of*

Man, p. 263: "Like the Omega which attracts it . . ." *The Singularities of The Human Species* (1955), p. 46.

16. "L'Energie humaine" (1956; *L'Energie humaine,* p. 183).

17. This is how a colleague and contemporary of Fr. Teilhard spoke of metaphysics: Pedro Descoqs, *Le mystère de notre élévation surnaturelle* (Paris, 1938), p. 97.

18. See letter of April 29, 1934, to Fr. de Lubac, concerning "two kinds of knowledge": ". . . I mistrust metaphysics (in the usual sense of the word) because I suspect it may be a geometry. But I am ready to recognize another sort of metaphysics which would be actually a hyperphysics—or a hyperbiology" (in *Choisir* [April, 1965], p. 18).

19. "La centrologie," no. 25 (*L'Activation de l'énergie,* p. 119).

20. *Science et Christ,* p. 208.

21. See, for example, the second part of "Comment je crois" (1934). See also *Teilhard de Chardin, the Man and His Meaning,* Part II, in particular pp. 180 and 202.

22. Again on January 5, 1955, the year of his death, Fr. Teilhard defined the Revelation as "the beyond manifesting itself 'personally' to earthly life": "Barrière de la mort et coréflexion," Appendix: "Science et Révélation" (*L'Activation de l'énergie,* p. 427). Is this an "ascent" or a "descent"?

23. "Forma Christi" (*Ecrits,* p. 341), etc.

24. *L'Activation de l'énergie,* pp. 152–157.

25. *The Divine Milieu,* pp. 50–51.

26. *The Divine Milieu,* pp. 85, 61, 114, 116–117, and 132. "Forma Christi" (*Ecrits,* pp. 339–342). Retreat of 1940. See *Teilhard de Chardin, the Man and His Meaning,* pp. 13–19.

27. *The Divine Milieu,* pp. 74 and 138.

28. Letter of February 2, 1916 (*The Making of a Mind,* p. 93).

29. *The Divinie Milieu,* p. 112.

30. *Ecrits du temps de la guerre,* pp. 161–162 and 167 (August 13, 1917).

31. "Science et Christ" (*Science et Christ* 58–59).

32. Letter to Léontine Zanta, January 25, 1924.

33. "Mon univers" (1924; *Science et Christ,* pp. 78–91). See "La foi qui opère" (1918; *Ecrits,* p. 322). *The Phenomenon of Man,* p. 270.

34. "Comment je vois" (1948), no. 14. *The Phenomenon of Man,* etc. Also see the texts cited in *Pensée religieuse,* pp. 106–114. *La vision du passé,* pp. 232–233.

35. N. Wildiers, *Teilhard de Chardin* (Paris, 1960), p. 44. Fr. Maurice Corvez was inspired by the Teilhardian conception and summarized it in his little book, *De la science à la foi, Teilhard de Chardin* (Paris, 1965).

36. "Le phénomène humain" (1928; *Science et Christ,* p. 127). See *The Phenomenon of Man,* p. 189: "The pre-eminent dignity and axial value of our species"; etc. "L'Esprit de la terre" (*L'Energie humaine,* p. 52).

37. *Man's Place in Nature.*

38. *The Phenomen of Man* (1928) (*Science et Christ,* p. 126).

39. "La place de l'homme dans la nature" (1933; *La vision du passé,* p. 255).

40. *The Phenomenon of Man,* p. 33. He did not hesitate to speak (*ibid.,* p. 284) of certain prejudices of science. "Comment je crois" (1934). "Sauvons l'humanité, réflexions sur la crise présente" (1936; *Science et Christ,* pp. 173–175).

41. "La place de l'homme dans l'univers, réflexions sur la complexité" (1942; *La vision du passé,* p. 318). "Comment je vois" (1948), no. 7.

42. "La réflexion de l'énergie" (1952; *L'Activation de l'énergie,* p. 340).

43. *Science et Christ,* p. 128.

44. *Annales de Paleontologie,* t. 41, 1955, p. 5. (Introduction) and p. 51 (Conclusion).

45. Address commemorating the tenth anniversary of the death of Fr. Pierre Teilhard de Chardin, and delivered April 10, 1965, in the auditorium of the French Broadcasting System in Paris. Etienne Gilson, *loc. cit.,* p. 725, also recognized this function of Teilhard's thought: "The central aim of his thought

is to throw light on the particular and eminent place of man in the whole of evolution, etc." In our opinion the author could have laid more stress on the originality of the arguments Teilhard used for putting across this great fact.

46. *The Phenomenon of Man,* p. 101.

47. He is speaking here of the text published in November, 1930, in the *Revue des questions scientifiques* (Louvain-Brussels), reproduced in *La vision du passé,* pp. 227–243. Another essay bearing the same title preceded it in 1928 (*Science et Christ,* pp. 115–128), itself preceded by "L'Hominisation" in 1925 (*La vision du passé,* pp. 75–112). Jean Pivetau compared these texts in his *Teilhard de Chardin savant* (1964). The fundamental idea was often developed in other works, such as in *The Phenomenon of Man, Man's Place in Nature,* and *The Singularities of the Human Species.* See *Man's Place,* Introduction: "In the initial stages of science (practically the entire nineteenth century) man was able to delve into whole worlds while taking *himself* quite for granted. Isn't this an instance of 'not being able to see the forest for the trees' or of not feeling the majesty of the ocean for the waves?, etc."

48. See *Pensée religieuse,* pp. 230–231. However, this text should not be taken to mean that Teilhard had simply rejected "Einstein's universe." Elsewhere, for example, he pointed out a certain analogy between two forms of "the space-time," that of Einsteinian physics and that of biology: *The Phenomenon of Man,* p. 84; *Man's Place in Nature.* In "Du cosmos à la cosmogénèse" (1951) he spoke of a "['hyper-Einsteinian'] space-time" (*L'Activation de l'énergie,* p. 265). In "Comment je vois" (1948), no. 9, he asks us to "adopt, in the case of very big complexes, a 'non-Euclidean geo- (or bio-)metry,' if we can put it that way, —that is, a biology with *n* new dimensions."

49. *Pensée religieuse,* pp. 240–241. "L'Esprit de la terre" (*L'Energie humaine,* pp. 26 and 30). Etienne Borne in his *De Pascal à Teilhard de Chardin* also shows the similarity between the two men with regard to this point.

50. "Positivist science, through three centuries of uninter-

rupted progress, has ruined" the Christian conception of the universe, etc. Around 1925, Fr. Desbuquois told us that one of the most important tasks ahead is the writing of a work to answer Séailles.

51. Nor do the formulas on the "Christogenesis," or other analogies. We can say this without reducing their scope. A recent work asks us to consider the two sentences which follow, one taken from "La vie cosmique" (cited in *The Future of Man,* p. 305), the other from "Note on Progress" (1920; *The Future of Man,* p. 22: "And since the time when Jesus was born, when He finished growing and died and rose again, *everything has continued to move forward because Christ has not yet completed His own forming.*" "Christ, as we know fulfils Himself gradually through the ages in the sum of our individual endeavors." Had the author of this work noted the phrase "as we know," he would have realized that he was merely transcribing a general truth known to all. Clearly, Teilhard was talking about the completion of the "Mystical Body." The lines immediately following the first sentence testify to this. "Christ has not yet gathered in the last folds of His robe, the robe of flesh and love which His faithful are making for Him. *The mystical Christ is not yet full-grown.*" (Teilhard's italics.) The lines preceding and following the second sentence indicate the same thing. "Neither we nor our adversaries have an adequate picture of the developments Christ has assigned His Church"; ". . . complete the Body of Christ." The author of this work has not been any more successful with the many other sentences he has quoted and commented upon.

52. *Science et Christ,* p. 58. In "La lutte contre la multitude" he said, "The real effort of evolution is preserved and carried forward by evangelic sainthood, not by the forces of pride" (*Ecrits,* p. 127). Is this what one would call a "humanitarian Prometheism"?

53. *Faith in Man* (1947; *The Future of Man,* pp. 188–189). "La mystique de la science" (1939; *L'Energie humaine,* p. 223). "A Note on Progress" (1920; *The Future of Man,* p. 19), etc.

166

See *supra,* note 29. "La vie cosmique" (*Ecrits,* p. 25) would have us "follow Prometheus' example" but only with respect to the earth, that we might "master and harness matter." See Pierre Smulders, S.J., *The Vision de Teilhard de Chardin* (Westminster, 1967).

54. "L'Hominisation" (*La vision du passé,* p. 96); "Why not ask Man himself to explain the mammals to us?" (p. 97), etc. "L'Esprit de la terre": "Everything takes on form and is clarified in him" (*L'Energie humaine,* p. 30).

55. "Recherche, travail, et adoration," March, 1955 (*Science et Christ,* p. 283).

56. "Le phénomène humain" (1930) (*La vision du passé,* pp. 235–239). "La convergence de l'univers" (1951; *L'Activation de l'énergie,* p. 303). "Le Christique" (January, 1955), p. 3, etc.

57. "L'Esprit de la terre" (*L'Energie humaine,* p. 29). "Le phénomène humain" (1928) (*Science et Christ,* p. 126). See "Comment je vois" (1948), no. 4. Teilhard goes from "cosmology" to "anthropology" to wind up in "theology." But he does not, like some authors who even sometimes manage to influence believers, reduce theology to anthropology.

58. *The Phenomenon of Man,* p. 163.

59. "La place de l'homme dans l'univers" (1942; *La vision du passé,* p. 324). See *supra,* note 12.

60. "L'Esprit de la terre" (1933; *L'Energie humaine,* pp. 53 and 55). "Adoration" is "the greatest act of fidelity to Being" (p. 47).

61. "Comment je vois" (1934), second section. "L'Esprit de la terre" (*L'Energie humaine,* p. 54).

62. See "Comment je vois" (1948), no. 37.

63. For the "happiness to adore" see "Réflexions sur le bonheur," in *Cahiers Pierre Teilhard de Chardin,* vol. 2, p. 64. "L'Atomisme de l'esprit": "All morality borders on adoration" (*L'Activation de l'énergie,* p. 60). For him the "Christian phenomenon" is basically a phenomenon of "adoration": "Le Christique" (1955). See *The Making of a Mind,* pp. 68, 79. In

"L'Esprit de la terre" he salutes the dawn "of the explicit triumph of adoration" (*L'Energie humaine,* p. 54). See "Mon univers" (1924; *Science et Christ,* p. 103), where he speaks of "the celestial Jerusalem" where "there will be nothing left to see but the rays of God's glory materialized in us."

Homily

FOR THE MASS OF THE TENTH ANNIVERSARY
OF THE DEATH OF PIERRE TEILHARD DE CHARDIN
DELIVERED BY FATHER ANDRÉ RAVIER
AT SAINT IGNACE'S CHURCH
PARIS, MARCH 25, 1965

Ten years . . . ten years have passed since that day in April, 1955, when the news of Pierre Teilhard de Chardin's sudden death flashed over the wires from New York. We are gathered here tonight as a community of souls transcending all vain dispute and bound in fidelity to a marvelous friendship. And we, his friends, still feel the sorrow we felt on that day. We feel it in our hearts and in our lives, for it is a wound that does not heal with time. You will recall that he died on Easter Sunday. Surely we can say that this was a day he would have chosen in his heart. Yet he would have preferred Good Friday (as we know from an entry in his journal dating two days earlier). For as he put it, it was the "predestined day" and belonged to the "crucified God, who, through His crucifixion, is the most powerful spiritual force behind 'ultra-hominisation' since He is the most sustaining and only redeeming force." And he added, "This is my faith; how much I would like to be able to confess it publicly before I die." Two days after expressing this wish he passed on.

But this is precisely what his writings have done. People all over the world are seeking faith; their thirst for it is greater than their thirst for science, despite what they say. Teilhard's faith, his spiritual experience, has made a strong impression on them, and they are thinking about it and talking it over. "On certain days," he wrote, "the sea brightens only when a ship

169

or a swimmer cuts through it. Similarly, the world brightens with God's presence only in response to our movement within it." This was prophetic of his own destiny. For ten years now, the world has been responding to his movement. He opens man's heart as a prow cuts through the sea. Man is taking a fresh look at the problem of God, seeing it in new perspectives and in new terms. He is enlightened, and even if his heart should close again in dark refusal, as sometimes happens, still he will never be quite the same. This astonishing change is reflected in articles and books, conferences and discussions, and it will mark our times as a decisive period in the history of mystic Catholicism.

As his works are read, Fr. Teilhard is better known for the person he really was. But are we, his friends, wholly satisfied? Have our expectations been fulfilled? Here, tonight, those who knew him well, those who loved him, recall a Teilhard bearing little resemblance to the person now becoming known as the Teilhard of history. We know that the private person, the inner man, has not yet been "grasped" by literature. Moreover, perhaps he is ungraspable. In the dramatic years between 1950 and 1955 he retired into silence as his situation was being reviewed. (It was not evasion or secrecy—could it have been modesty?) He withdrew into silence as though, deep within himself, he regained a world known and accessible to him alone, a world beyond the quarrels of men, beyond academic controversies, a world where he rediscovered his truth, his liberty, his light— what he would have called "his precious nappes of divine energy." Soon his face was to radiate a strange peace; it was to reflect forgiveness and certainty, the suffering he had overcome, and the pain he had taken upon himself.

Tonight, let us take a few moments to try to approach the inner mystery of Fr. Teilhard de Chardin. We do so with infinite respect and with the realization that our words cannot possibly encompass him. Perhaps we will be able to hear the "unique note" he spoke of in his writings, the note "which sustains and dominates (all sounds created), the note in which all the powers of [his] soul, in response to God, begin to resonate."

The inner mystery of Teilhard! Or rather, the mystery of God in Teilhard's soul. We believe that Christian mysticism summons a man to live in the innermost recesses of his soul, in the vibration of all the powers of his being, and in his most human and tender sensibility, his love of Jesus Christ; it will have him refuse in his heart, like Paul the Apostle and John the Evangelist, to separate Jesus from Jesus of Nazareth, and from Christ the Pleroma of the world. And if this is what constitutes Christian mysticism, then Teilhard was a true mystic. In the luminous lines on the communion of his mass, we find a subdued, original, yet faithful echo of the Epistle to the Ephesians and the prologue to the Fourth Gospel: "Lost in the mystery of the divine flesh, I cannot say which of the two beatitudes is the most radiant, to have found the Word in order to dominate matter, or to possess matter in order to attain and undergo the light of God."

How did he live this passionate love for Jesus Christ? We do not learn the answer without some surprise. Teilhard was usually vitally and jealously interested in seeing the world progress towards its highest state of being, carrying this interest so far that he made action, particularly the select action 'research,' into a duty, a sacred human duty. Nevertheless, if we read him carefully, he sometimes seemed to be concerned solely with the pure values of grace, the spiritual quality of souls. Let us examine the moving apostrophe which he addressed to his sister Marguerite who had just died after a long life of suffering. "Oh Marguerite, my sister, as I journeyed across continents and seas, dedicated to the positive forces of the universe, passionately caught up in watching all the colors of the earth rise, you, immobile and supine, struggled with the worst shadows of the world and, there, in your innermost self, metamorphosed them into light. Tell me, which of us has conducted himself best in the eyes of the Creator?" What a diptych! What an intimate confession! What a brilliant flash from his innermost self! And where does he see the true light shining? On a poor sick woman whose "immobile action" prevails over the precious activity of

171

researchers, workers, artisans, and all the builders of the world
. . . and this, in the eyes of the Creator!

Tonight, the twenty-fifth of March, it is fitting that we reread
what Teilhard has written about the Annunciation. Here, as elsewhere, his words glow with the warmth which illuminates his
language whenever he speaks of the Virgin Mary. "God chose
a time when He would manifest Himself before us in the flesh.
And when that time came, he had to establish a virtue in the
world capable of drawing Himself to us. He needed a mother
to deliver Him into the human sphere. And what did He do? He
created the Virgin Mary, that is, He created on earth a purity
so great that He was able to center Himself in its transparency
until the little Child appeared." Is purity, like suffering, basically an active virtue, one which metamorphoses the world?
We know how Teilhard answered this question in his soul.

We must go a step further and look into the anguish and
inner bewilderment in his heart. For his faith in the world
sprang from these depths, as did that quality we call by a
highly ambiguous term, "his optimism."

He was always fearful of the meaninglessness of certain de-
feats, of suffering, of death, of all that he called the passivities
of diminishment. But more than that, existence itself filled him
with horror. As far back as 1923 he maintained that "it is a
terrible thing to be born, to find oneself, without having desired
it, irrevocably swept up in a torrent of energy which seems to
want to destroy everything it is bearing along in its current."
This is truly the spiritual experience of the void, his void, and
he experienced it each time he "took up the lamp and left what
seemed to be the lighted area of [his] activities and daily affairs, to [go down into] the innermost recesses of himself."
There he experienced what he called "the distress of an atom
lost in the universe." This is the anguish of Teilhard. This world
that he loved, this world whose principle he wanted to adore,
this world overwhelmed him from the start. "Like every man,
I have an instinctive desire to pitch my tent on a choice summit.
And like my brothers I am afraid of a future which duration
forces me to enter and which promises too much mystery and

too much newness. And then I ask myself, anxious with the rest of them, where life is going . . ."

But his faith takes a desperate leap and banishes his fear. "If anything saved me, it was the sound of the evangelic voice guaranteed through divine successes, speaking to me out of the depths of my night, calling, 'It is I, do not fear.' O my God, I throw myself upon your Word." There is doubtless nothing more essential in the psychology of the mystic than to feel oneself suspended above the abyss of one's void, held by nothing but the thin invisible thread of one's faith in Christ. Teilhard had this feeling strongly. It led him to work hard towards establishing a balance between "a constant openness" and "a steadfast detachment"; as a man of science he needed to love the world in order to better explore its countenance; as a son—a most loyal son of Ignatius Loyola—he understood that the self must continually die in order to live in God. It is true, is it not, that he only achieved this balance through a costly and fragile dialectic? It seems that the only way his soul could really regain its joy was through accepting, in faith, the anguish man feels in the face of evil and death.

Finally, if we see it in its true psychological context, we are glimpsing the secret of Teilhard's joy. This joy is also of a mystical character. It stems more from his being possessed by God than from his possessing Him. And it is significant that he derived this joy from the Eucharist and from death, not from the earth. The earth betrays those who love it; not from the earth, unless it be that earth which has been sanctified by the Incarnation, whose bread and wine has been transubstantiated into the body and blood of Christ by the words and actions of the priest—not from the earth unless it be that earth that is his body now returned to dust, now reduced to nothing, one day to rise again with the resurrected Christ, in the resurrected Christ. "Lord," he prayed, "enclose me in the deepest entrails of your heart, and when you are holding me there, burn me, purify me, inflame me, transfigure me to the perfect satisfaction of your tastes, to the utter annihilation of myself." Has any man, even those who have attained the most complete mystical

173

negativities, ever addressed Jesus Christ with a more moving appeal?

This brings us to a clearer understanding of the phrase which closes his letter of Good Friday, 1955: ". . . the crucified God, who, through His crucifixion, is the most powerful spiritual force behind 'ultra-hominisation' since He is the most sustaining and only redeeming force . . . This is my faith." His faith. A faith in the inestimable value of the Cross. A faith which is also a love. A personal love, a passionate love of Him whom he, like Paul and like John, liked to address simply and tenderly as Jesus. Listen to his cry. *"Jesus solus, solus Jesus"*: "Jesus alone, only Jesus!" And how he loved Him! During one of his retreats he wrote, "Entirely suspended to Him, in my cohesion, my action, even in my perception of and passion for Him." This is so true that his spiritual crises—he had several and they were serious ones—all seem at some point to be moments of extreme tension between his love of "Jesus" and his love of the Christ-Pleroma of the world. But despite the "distress" which he admits having felt at times during his "retreat into God alone," in the end it was always the personal love of Jesus which triumphed. "Lord Jesus, I submit to being possessed by you, to being united with your Body and led through its inexpressible power towards solitudes I would have never dared set out for alone."

"I submit." This is the "yes" of his deep soul, the secret "yes" he spoke to Jesus again and again throughout his life, regardless of what befell him; for in the annihilation of his innermost self he sought the transfiguration of his research and his action, of his love of man and the earth. And thus he was magnificently gathered into the law which has conditioned all spiritual causation since the Incarnation and the Annunciation: if the Word of God is to descend into flesh and to live among us, if He is to metamorphose the world through His presence, there must be a soul whose purity calls and receives Him.

Amen.